Chronicles of Moses משה

Scharl van Sladen TRM

Artwork done by Throne Room Mystic

All images generated using AI - ChatGPT image creator

Typesetting/layout - Seraph Creative

First Edition: January 2025

ISBN: 978-1-964959-36-8

eBook: 978-1-964959-37-5

Published by Seraph Creative in 2025

United States / United Kingdom / South Africa / Australia

www.seraphcreative.org

Bible references used from The NIV Translation, The Amplified Version and The Passion Translation.

TABLE OF CONTENTS

Thank you

To the Lover of my soul, Jesus — You rock.

To my dear friends, Justin and Rachel Abraham, and the entire COBH team: Your pioneering spirit, determination, and unwavering commitment to building the mystic nation are truly inspiring. A big thank you — I continue to learn so much from you.

To my students at the Throne Room Mystic Academy: Your support made this book, and many more to come, possible. Thank you for believing in me.

To my four wonderful kids: You are a weird bunch, and I love you endlessly.

To my wife, Bianca: Thank you for believing in me and encouraging me to press forward. I love you with all my heart.

FOREWORD

We are in the age of the mysteries of heaven being fully revealed to hungry hearts. A time of profound expansion of knowledge and understanding, the age of wisdom and light. To help us transition into the next age, God is releasing clear voices, oracles and forerunners to help pave the way forward. Scharl van Staden is one of those chosen voices. Scharl is an authentic representative of the Spirit of Christ, a guide to take us beyond the superficial into the substance. Using deep knowledge of ancient Jewish mysticism, biblical understanding and direct revelation from Christ, Scharl has written a substantial book that will trigger Divine bliss, a book that will awaken your capacity to ascend and transcend the limitations of our time. A book made for deep meditation, contemplation and bliss-filled study. A book that will open up your awareness to the realms of the Spirit and invite you into the place of wonder. This is an instant mystical classic. Thank you Scharl for sharing this with book us. I know it's going to be a significant blessing to so many people.

Justin Paul Abraham
Company of Burning Hearts
COBH.live

INTRODUCTION

Humanity has crossed the threshold of a profound spiritual awakening, echoing that we are more than traditional Christianity has revealed. The concept of spiritual ascension, as presented in this book, is an invitation to reconnect with our primordial existence, unlocking dimensions of understanding that resonate with the frequency of Yahweh's breath. This journey mirrors Moses' ascent on Mount Sinai, where boundaries dissolve, revealing the celestial paths of divine intention and substance.

The Matrix of Ascension emerges as a cosmic blueprint—a multidimensional field where Yahweh's creative force flows, transforming spirit into matter. This matrix is the divine womb, the vessel of creation, where infinite potential crystallises into manifest reality. Within its sacred geometry lies the framework through which the sons of God reclaim their divine heritage, awakening their spiritual DNA to ascend into realms of divine consciousness.

The life of Moses serves as a luminous model for this transformative process. Born a Hebrew child raised as Egyptian royalty—his journey encapsulates the archetypal path of ascension. From his encounter with Yahweh at the burning bush to his transfiguration on Mount Sinai, Moses reveals the potential for humanity to ascend beyond earthly limitations, guided by the breath of Yahweh. His name, Moshe משה, encoded with the elements of water (mem מ), fire (shin ש), and breath (hey ה), reflects the alchemical process of ascension, where the earthly is consumed by the divine, and the human spirit is clothed in heavenly garments.

The Mystery of Ascension, in the Hebrew Words, drives the transformation of consciousness, which is the core of this journey. The Hebrew terms La, Nasa, and Salak represent ascending phases of spiritual maturity. La (לה) signifies divine breath guiding us through dimensions. Nasa (נשא) embodies the lifting power that echoes in our DNA, and Salak (סלק) leads to celestial governance. Together, they form a sacred spiral, unveiling our primordial identity as divine co-creators with Yahweh.

The Multi-Dimensional Garments described in Hebrew mysticism are key to navigating these realms. As Moses ascended, he was clothed in spiritual garments woven from the fabric of divine light, enabling his transformation into a vessel of Yahweh's glory. These garments are not merely symbolic but vibrational interfaces that align the spirit with higher dimensions, aligning communion with the heavenly realms.

INTRODUCTION

The Measuring Phase, a journey of introspection and healing, reveals the importance of emotional and spiritual wholeness as the foundation for ascension. As we are weighed and measured, old paradigms fall away, and we are clothed with the authority and wisdom to govern creation in alignment with Yahweh's purpose. Healing is not just restoration, but a divine recalibration that prepares us to ascend into our true identity.

Through the practice of ascension, we engage with the Realms of Spiritual Entities, stepping into the divine council as Moses did on Mount Horeb. This sacred assembly of heavenly beings, described in scriptures such as Psalm 82 and Daniel 7, represents the convergence of earthly and celestial realms. Interacting with angels and divine messengers enhances our understanding of Yahweh's intricate governance and aligns us with our role as co-creators in the divine plan.

Finally, the Concept of Transcendence encapsulates the essence of ascension: the surpassing of physical boundaries to dwell in the heart of Yahweh. As the Apostle Paul described in 2 Corinthians 12, ascension unveils inexpressible mysteries and activates divine transformation. In this elevated state, we not only return to our original state but also gain the authority to rule over creation as Yahweh's sons and daughters, fulfilling the promise of Romans 8:19 that creation eagerly anticipates the revelation of God's sons.

The Ascension Matrix of Moses is not merely a theoretical framework but a living reality, an invitation to step into the fullness of our divine purpose. It calls us to ascend, to remember, and to govern—to bridge heaven and earth as the radiant sons of Yahweh, clothed in light and crowned with the authority of divine love.

The purpose of this book is not to get through it, but to get lost in it. Each topic or realm creates a space for contemplation and meditation to fully grasp the mysteries and treasures hidden within.

Using both biblical and mystical texts with the Hebrew language as foundation, I've created a basis for you to enter the gateways of the Mysteries of Ascension. May this book arrest your spirit and catapult you into new dimensions of your sonship.

THE CONCEPT OF SPIRITUAL ASCENSION

LIVING BEYOND

In the sacred dance between spirit and divinity, ascension emerges as the divine blueprint for the sons of God to return to its primordial state or original intent.

Paraphrasing the **Zohar** "When the Holy One, blessed be He, created man, He made him in the likeness of the upper realms. He gathered dust from the four corners of the world and formed it into the body of man. Then He breathed into him the breath of life from the supernal source, and man became a living being. This breath connected him to the divine, endowing him with a soul that reflected the heavenly realms. Thus, man was created with both an earthly form and a heavenly essence, linking the physical and spiritual worlds, making him unique among all creatures."

Like Moses, who ascended Mount Sinai, enveloped in the garment of God's presence, we too are called to traverse the heights of spiritual consciousness that stretch far beyond our material understanding. This journey isn't merely a spiritual exercise—it is the essence of our restoration as sons of Yahweh, an entanglement of remembrance, sparking our eternal connection to Yahweh preceding creation itself.

From within the chambers of this celestial ascent lies a transformation that ignites the structure of our primordial existence. As you step into higher dimensions of spiritual awareness, your DNA awakens to its divine coding, a matrix, activating what the ancients and sages called our light body—the glorified form that resonates with heavenly frequencies.

Mystical writings reveal that "The righteous ascend by known paths and ways to the supernal light that shines."

This profound metamorphosis echoes through Psalm 89's revelation of the divine council, where sons of God commune with celestial beings in the courts of heaven.

Just as a ladder bridges earth and heaven, the path of ascension creates sacred corridors between realms, allowing divine energy to flow unimpeded between our earthly existence and the higher dimensions. This isn't a distant concept but a living reality where the sons of God, through their relationship with Christ, can access the multi-dimensional aspects of creation. Here, we don't just meet wisdom, but get entangled in her, as layers of divine consciousness unveil the expansive awareness of our true nature in Yahweh.

As you mature in this journey, you'll release the dense patterns of lower frequencies, expanding into true resonance with the image of God. Your awareness stretches beyond the limited constructs of material existence into the vast ocean of divine understanding, where you discover your interconnectedness with all of creation. In this sacred space, you don't just see the divine council—we take our rightful place within it, participating in the governance of creation through Christ.

This elevation of consciousness is a collective restoration of your divine heritage. Through Jesus, the firstborn, we gain access to realms where angels ascend and descend, where divine wisdom flows freely, and gods and thrones entangle in governance. This is the true nature of ascension—home in the heart of the Father.

THE MATRIX OF ASCENSION

The Matrix (Racham רחם) embodies the fundamental fabric of the spirit, functioning as both the generative womb of creation and the interconnected field through which existence manifests. As a spiritual construct, it serves as the interface between infinite and finite realms, where formless spirituality crystallises into manifest substance.

Mystical writings describing the concept of *racham* (רחם), or the "womb" of creation as the supernal point, when it expanded within, prepared a palace for itself, a sacred space in which it would dwell. This palace is the womb (*racham*), wherein the seeds of creation were implanted and nurtured. From this womb, the light flowed forth, illuminating all realms and creating the worlds above and below. This womb holds within it the mysteries of the beginning, where the first stirrings of existence took form. It is here that God, sowed the seeds of life and potential, from which all creation would emerge. Thus, the womb became the foundation of the worlds, the hidden source that nourishes and sustains all being.

This ascension grid of infinite possibilities acts as both container and catalyst, facilitating the emergence of scrolls and mandates into physical reality.

The Matrix operates as a multidimensional grid of consciousness, connecting you to an intricate web of energy, frequency and information of the heavenly realms. It mediates between thought and manifestation, spirit and matter, potential and actualisation. This field exhibits holographic properties, with each point containing the informational blueprint of the whole, enabling interconnected resonance and synchronistic ecstasies of the image of Yahweh.

As a container of potentiality, the Matrix holds all possible expressions of His image before manifestation, acting as a cosmic womb nurturing spiritual development. It bridges spiritual and material realms while facilitating the transformation of the maturity of the sons of God. This transformative aspect enables consciousness expansion through alchemical processes, like the Hebrew letters, transmuting potential into manifest form.

The Matrix functions as the infrastructure through which consciousness interacts with reality, enabling intentional manifestation and orchestrating experience. It serves as both foundation and medium through which all creation and creative potential emerge into substance.

The Matrix of Ascension רחם is the divine womb where infinite potential crystallises into manifest reality through divine consciousness. It is the multidimensional grid through which

Yahweh's creative force flows, transforming spirit into matter through sacred Hebrew geometries like the Hebrew letters.

This cosmic infrastructure serves as both container and catalyst, where heaven interfaces with earth, enabling the sons of God to mature into their divine image.

MOSES' ASCENSION AS A MODEL

Moses' journey up Mount Sinai is a powerful example of the transformative process of ascension. Throughout this book, we will journey through the encounters and dimensional processes that Moses ascended to unlock the frequency realms of Yahweh as his spirit underwent a change of spiritual garments absorbing the essence of divine frequency.

In **Exodus 19:3**, Moses went up to God and received a call from the Lord. This moment signified the awakening of His spirit and a profound encounter with the path of ascension.

By journeying through the realms of wonder פלא, through the Hebrew term 'בּיא', which we will delve into later, Moses discovered the key to unlocking Yahweh's DNA ladder. This allowed his consciousness to merge with the mountain of his potential as leader, ruler, governor and co-creator.

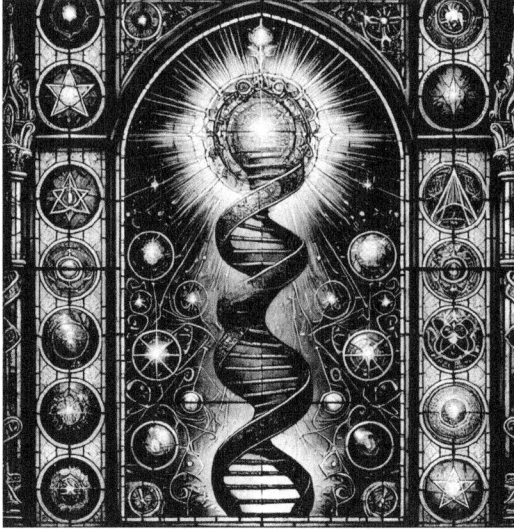

PRACTICAL THOUGHTS ON ASCENSION

VARIED EXPERIENCES OF SEEING

The concept of "seeing" shouldn't be confined to one definition. I've had conversations with numerous people who desire to vividly experience the spiritual realm through their physical sight and limit it to that desire. Unfortunately, many find themselves unable to move forward in their seeing because of that. If they don't view it from that perspective, then they simply believe they are not seeing. By disregarding the practice of seeing unless it's vividly, with your physical eyes, you are doing a disservice to your spiritual encounter. The practice of embracing the skill of applying your imagination can lead to surprising discoveries and a heightened spiritual connection. I take what I perceive and enhance it with my imagination.

Don't allow the ability to see hinder you. Some individuals may have a more visual encounter during ascension, where they actually perceive images or landscapes in the heavenly realms. However, others may have a more intuitive or sensory experience, where they feel or sense the presence and energy of the heavenly realms without seeing them with their physical eyes. Don't get discouraged if your ability to see differs from others. Ascension is a personal journey, and everyone's experience will be unique to them. It is about unlocking and unpacking our position as sons and daughters of God, tapping into the spiritual realm, engaging with Jesus. By doing so, we can deepen our understanding of our identity, our purpose, and our relationship with the Father.

So, rather than focusing on the limitation of sight, embrace the different ways in which you can engage with the heavenly realms and allow the transformative power of ascension to shape your spiritual journey.

Some individuals perceive things in a visual manner, almost like watching a video, whereas others may have a more abstract perception. The ability to imagine plays a crucial role, as it can shape your experience. Imagination creates reality.

Here's an example of how I see in the spirit? I sense presence. I am aware of the presence of angelic realms enveloping me, which includes specific angels or individuals from the cloud of witnesses.

I use my imagination and connect it to my spiritual senses to perceive things in the spiritual realm.

I don't see in the spirit the way I look at you. Surprisingly, a handful perceive the spiritual realm in that way. In fact, the majority of people perceive it the way I've just stated. I apply my imagination to what I sense. After all, that's exactly why you have an imagination, it's your canvas of the spirit realm. Therefore, it is important not to confine or limit your understanding of spiritual seeing to a narrow definition, but to embrace the vast possibilities that exist within the realm of spirituality.

In the rich tradition of Hebrew mysticism, there is a hierarchy of visual realms that transcends physical sight. This system describes six distinct levels of seeing, each representing a deeper connection to spiritual understanding and divine wisdom. I added it as an extra but will not be a focus point of this book.

The most basic level is Ra'ah (ראה), which encompasses our physical sight and recognition of the material world. While fundamental, it holds within it the seeds of deeper perception, serving as the gateway to higher forms of understanding.

Moving deeper, we encounter Chazah (חָזָה), the realm of prophetic vision. As described in the Zohar, this level enables one to perceive beyond physical reality, glimpsing future potentials and understanding divine patterns woven through existence.

Hibit (הִבִּיט) represents a profound shift into contemplative gazing, where seeing becomes a transformative act. This level integrates vision with being, creating a deep contemplative awareness that changes both the observer and the observed.

The level of Shur (שׁוּר) brings forth intuitive perception, manifesting as spiritual discernment and inner knowing. This form of seeing allows you to recognise subtle patterns and meanings that lie beneath surface appearances.

Tzafah (צָפָה) elevates seeing to a strategic and protective function, embodying a guardian consciousness. This watchful observation serves not just to perceive but to protect and guide, offering insights that help navigate both spiritual and material realms.

Finally, we reach Ashar (אָשַׁר), the level of validated seeing. Rooted in the concept of confirmation, this highest form represents verified and authorised perception. It's a seeing that has been tested and confirmed, carrying with it the weight of authentic spiritual truth.

These levels of perception form a ladder of spiritual ascent, each rung offering a deeper understanding of both the visible and invisible aspects of reality. Through this system, Hebrew mysticism provides a framework for developing not just sharper vision, but profound wisdom and spiritual insight.

Baal Shem Tov on Seeing and Mystical Progression:

The Baal Shem Tov taught that these levels of seeing form a ladder of consciousness:

1. Physical Sight (Ra'ah) - Seeing with physical eyes
2. Enhanced Awareness (Shur) - Seeing patterns and connections
3. Watchful Observation (Tzafah) - Seeing with protective awareness
4. Contemplative Gazing (Hibit) - Seeing with transformative intent
5. Prophetic Vision (Chazah) - Seeing beyond time
6. Validated Seeing (Ashar) - Seeing with divine confirmation
7. Unified Perception - Seeing all levels simultaneously

Activate your levels of seeing by following the exercise in Ascension activations at the end of the book.

3 Enoch 45:1: "I saw what he saw, I perceived what he perceived, and I knew what he knew."

The Merkavah tradition adds that each level of seeing corresponds to a different heavenly palace, requiring appropriate preparation and purification to access. Our purification and access lies in the finished work of the cross.

From the concepts of the Zohar regarding the progressive nature of spiritual vision:

"Each level of seeing opens another gate in the heavens, and with each gate, the soul is drawn closer to the hidden light. As one ascends through these gates, greater mysteries are revealed, and the soul is refined by the radiance it beholds. When the soul reaches the highest level, there is no longer a distinction between the one who sees and what is seen. All separation dissolves, and seeing and being become one. In that state, the soul is fully united with the divine light, perceiving without boundaries, as all veils are lifted, and it rests in the secret of the Infinite."

WOW, WOW, WOW, WOW !!!!!!!!!!!!!

ADAPTABILITY IN ASCENSION

It's important to be mindful of this during ascension, as some become fixated on their own perspectives and desires, hindering their ability to progress and resulting in a constant sense of dissatisfaction. They constantly have an experience of not seeing correctly. It's a repetitive emotion that evolves into a performance creating disappointment.

Keep in mind that ascension is a state of rest, where you lean into the breath and let the rhythm of Yahweh's breath guide you to different realms.

THE CONCEPT OF TRANSCENDENCE

Ascension is a transcendental experience. But what does that really mean? Many people associate anything related to the term "transcendental" with the new age movement. However, it's important to note that the concept of transcendence is not limited to any specific belief system or religion. Instead, it refers to going beyond physical boundaries and connecting with a higher level of consciousness or spirituality.

1 Enoch 71:1,5 "And it came to pass after this that my spirit was translated, And it ascended into the heavens... And the angel Michael seized me by my right hand, And lifted me up."

This idea is often linked to attaining higher levels of awareness and establishing connections with divine energies, entities, and frequencies within the image of Yahweh. When you ascend, you are essentially doing just that. Your existence goes beyond the limits of the physical realm, surpassing the restrictions of the senses. It allows you to expand your perceptions of visuals, sounds, and flavours into expanded dimensions. In this process, you overcome and transcend the limitations that once held you back.

2 Corinthians 12:2-4 "I know a man in Christ who fourteen years ago was caught up to the third heaven... was caught up to paradise and heard inexpressible things."

Transcendental activates divine transformation. The more you engage in ascension practices, the more your awareness expands. The more you develop your awareness, the more assured you become in your sensory abilities.

Mystical writings from the Zohar reveal that when a person's soul ascends at night, it traverses many firmaments, ascending and descending according to its deeds and purity. Each night, the soul is freed from the body to wander, encountering forces and witnessing mysteries that are hidden during the day. If it is found worthy, it ascends to behold the splendour of the upper worlds and to see what it sees. Such a soul is shown visions of light and knowledge, receiving wisdom that it may bring back upon waking. But if the soul is burdened by wrongdoing, it is restrained, wandering among shadows, unable to ascend to the higher realms. Therefore, the righteous soul delights in the mysteries of the night, while the soul of one who has transgressed remains troubled, bound to earthly matters.

Remember...read these verses of the Zohar from the finished work of the cross. We come from the realm of Shalom where all is accomplished for us and striving has ceased. We step in.

Your involvement, realms you engage, and encountering and interacting with the angelic. It is the elevation of the body and the soul's journey to increase the capacity to perceive and comprehend the divine mysteries. That's transcendental. It is an intensely personal and subjective experience, and each individual may have their own unique way of perceiving and experiencing the spiritual realm.

AN ASCENSION ACTIVATION BEFORE WE CONTINUE:

Take a comfortable position, relax and visualise Yahweh standing before you, and breathe in the breath of Yahweh. A breath into breath exchange. You can sense a surge of energy and life flowing through your being. Every cell in your body being awakened and revitalised. Exchanging breaths with Jesus transcends the physical realm, unveiling a deeper spiritual entanglement. You settle into your divine position in Him, enveloped in unlimited power and potential.

This awareness of your sonship in Christ propels you to a higher level of consciousness and authority. You comprehend the depth of what Moses experienced as he walked with God, and you hunger for that same level of intimacy and divine encounter.

This ascension journey is not about scraping the surface or settling for the basics; it's about unlocking the fullness of your identity and purpose in Christ.

As you embark on this journey, anticipate stepping into new dimensions of your sonship and experiencing the miraculous and supernatural as a new creation being, receiving divine revelation and instruction. The atmosphere at the table brims with anticipation and reverence. As you sit, you entangle Yahweh surrounding you, His divine energy pulsating through every fibre of your being. Each member of the divine council shares their wisdom and insights, unveiling profound mysteries and deep spiritual truths. The conversation flows effortlessly, positioning time in anticipation. The Holy Spirit imparts divine revelation, guiding you into a deeper understanding of your purpose and destiny. With His gentle and compassionate nature, Jesus imparts profound revelations on love and grace. Moses, imparts wisdom and insights of righteousness and justice. The Father, in His infinite wisdom, unveils the grand tapestry of creation and the intricate designs of the universe. As you listen and absorb the divine wisdom being poured out, your spirit soars with a newfound clarity and understanding.

As the ascension encounter concludes, you carry this divine entanglement with you, knowing the presence of Yahweh and the wisdom imparted on the sea of glass have forever transformed you.

" Through ascension, we awaken to our divine nature, unlocking the power and potential within to fulfil our primordial purpose and origins as sons of God."

THE MYSTERY OF ASCENSION IN THE HEBREW WORDS

Before we journey into the ascension matrix of Moses, we need to cover key Hebrew words linked to ascension and their relevance.

There are three Hebrew words that describe different phases of ascension.

THE FIRST HEBREW WORD IS LA לה.

Through לה, the divine breath of Yahweh guides you - this sacred Hebrew letter-pair encodes the very essence of divine respiration and spiritual elevation. Like the rhythmic pulse of creation itself, this breath moves through dimensions both seen and unseen, teaching you to navigate the subtle realms of the spirit. We are learning to ascend into realms of inheritance through the dimensions of His breath, each exchange drawing us higher, each exhalation releasing what no longer serves our elevation. This breath becomes your vehicle of ascension, a chariot of fire carrying consciousness through the veils of material existence into increasingly refined states of being. Through this divine respiration, you inherit not just promised lands of physical abundance, but entire dimensions of spiritual reality, each breath a key unlocking new territories of divine experience and understanding.

The word literally means **'to ascend, to lead out or to cause to rise'.** In its deepest essence, this represents an assisted ascension, where divine grace meets human intention in a sacred dance of elevation. As incense rises naturally toward heaven, seeking its source, so too does the spirit yearn for its heavenly unfolding.

It also means **'to offer a burnt offering'** - a transformation through sacred fire that purifies and transmutes the dense into the sublime. Jesus, who served as our ultimate sacrifice, paid the price that bridged the infinite gap between human limitation and divine potential. This cosmic transaction opened pathways previously sealed, creating channels of ascension through which consciousness can soar.

With confidence, we ascend and acknowledge ourselves as a pleasing offering to the Lord, like incense, well pleasing to Him. This sweet fragrance rises through the dimensions of creation, carrying our essence upward through the spheres of manifestation. In this mystical alchemy, we become both the offering and the offered, the ascended and the ascending, participating in a divine exchange that transcends ordinary understanding, an exchange the blood of Jesus initiated.

Another meaning is to **'increase in size'**, which I absolutely love. Oh, my goodness. That is exactly what happens as you ascend. You increase your capacity for experience, influence, and authority. Your consciousness unfolds like a cosmic flower, each realm revealing new dimensions of awareness. The boundaries of your former self dissolve as you expand into vast new territories of perception and understanding.

You unlock an awareness of a limitless spirit going beyond the boundary of physicality, discovering how consciousness itself has no walls, no ceiling, no floor. Like a drop of water merging with the ocean, you tap into the infinite expanse of your true nature. The small self who once felt confined to flesh and bone now breaches the edges of galaxies, dances with quantum possibilities, and communes with timeless wisdom permeating all existence.

This expansion echoes wherever you go, your gates influencing the atmosphere, not just in the spaces you physically occupy, but in the subtle realms that interpenetrate our material world. Your presence becomes a doorway through which higher frequencies can flow. People around you might not know why, but they sense the shift, the lightness, the peace, the subtle invitation to expand beyond their own perceived limitations. You become like a tuning fork, resonating at a frequency, awakening others to their own potential for transcendence, creating ripples of transformation extending far beyond your immediate sphere of influence.

The following additional meaning, **'To put into place'**, goes beyond mere physical positioning. It speaks to the extraordinary ability to traverse and anchor yourself across the infinite tapestry of existence. This is the art of dimensional fluidity, where consciousness flows like quicksilver between the veils of reality. You are, by nature, a multidimensional being - a cosmic crystalline structure with facets reflecting across countless realms of existence.

We are not just opening doors, we are dissolving the veil between dimensions, expanding our capacity to exist as conscious observers, bringing purpose and participants across the grand tapestry of creation. This multidimensional awakening is like learning to play a cosmic symphony, where each dimension is an instrument, and you are simultaneously the conductor and the orchestra.

The thought of this expansion fills me with awe and wonder. My spirit resonates with the ability of existing multidimensionally in the quantum dance of consciousness. To entangle the face of omnipresence is to understand our true nature as infinite beings. Levels of Light unfolding into Limitless Love!

Last, it means **'to be remembered'** - a profound truth that may be the primary key to ascension itself. This 'remembrance' isn't merely recollection, but a cosmic awakening to our primordial essence. When we connect with the spirit realm, we're not simply reaching outward, but inward to the deepest chambers of our eternal being. This connection evokes the luminous memory of our pre-creation existence within Yahweh - a state of pure, undifferentiated consciousness before the dawn of physical form.

Consider the sacred moment when Yahweh breathed life into a body crafted not of mere earth, but of radiant gold dust and living gemstones - each element holding specific frequencies of divinity. When Adam became a living being, it wasn't simply animation of flesh, but the embedding of heaven's memory into manifest form.

This divine breath carried within it the complete blueprint of our spiritual DNA, our divine purpose, and our eternal covenant.

The record of our primordial agreement with Yahweh - our original promise and purpose - still resonates within that first breath, echoing through the chambers of our cellular memory, encoded within the very essence of our being. Through the process of ascension, these ancient memories begin to stir and awaken. Like a flower opening to the dawn, each layer of awakening brings to light another facet of this eternal agreement that exists within Him. We're not just remembering - we're being remembered, a divine entanglement called back into alignment with our original resonance and purpose.

Remembrance is both a return and a revelation, showing who we were as primordial beings and how we function.

La לה is about revealing the identity of your position as a son of God.

As we journey from La לה to Nasa נשא, a beautiful choreography of spiritual ascension unfolds. In La לה, we gain enlightenment about our true essence as divine sons and daughters. It reveals the breath that propels us through various dimensions, elevating us to new heights. On the other hand, Nasa נשא captures the very essence of this elevation, as it symbolises the sacred lifting of consciousness, guiding us towards our purpose. This transition, from discovering our identity to actively ascending, mirrors the pattern of spiritual awakening. Once we recognise our divine nature, it naturally awakens our potential and ignites a desire to soar even higher.

THE SECOND HEBREW WORD IS NASA נשא.

Ezekiel 11:1 "The spirit lifted me up, brought me to the gate of the house of the Lord that faces east".

Nasa נשא, in its mystical depths, carries multiple layers of meaning - **'to carry'** ,**'to lift up'**, and **'a longing to go higher'**. It speaks to the eternal place in the hearts of man.

The 'lifting up' represents more than physical elevation, but a transformation of consciousness itself. It embodies the soul's perpetual desire to return to its celestial source, to break free from the constraints of material existence and soar into realms of pure spirit. This yearning is a part of our very nature, manifesting in cultures worldwide as the universal dream, the building of towers, and the exploration of the cosmos. We inherently are drawn to the adventure of exploration.

Then it means **'longing to go higher'**, points to an innate spiritual restlessness - a discontent with remaining static. It drives us to explore not only outer space, but inner space, the uncharted territories of awareness and being that lie embedded in the heavenly realms. Like ancient mystics ascending through the heavenly palaces (hechalot), or modern astronauts breaking free from earth's gravity, this primordial urge compels us to venture into unknown realms.

This concept reminds us that the desire to explore and transcend is not merely human ambition, but a divine spark within us, it's the voice of י Yod , an echo of the voice of Yahweh that drives all evolution and expansion in the universe. It suggests that our drive to reach beyond our current limitations is not just permitted, but mandated in our spiritual DNA, an encoding written by the Creator.

Nasa נשא is about revealing the eternity echoing in your DNA.

As we ascend from the lifting power of Nasa נשא, which reveals the eternal echoes in our DNA and our inherent drive toward transcendence, we also encounter an even deeper dimension of spiritual ascension through Salak סלק. While Nasa speaks to the divine spark of purpose that propels us upward, Salak introduces us to the transformative journey that awaits us in these higher realms.

This progression takes us from the initial purpose of spiritual elevation to the actual realms of celestial governance and dimensional authority. Just like a masterful symphony transitioning between movements, we shift our focus from the identity and purpose to ascend into the actual mechanics and mysteries of heavenly dimensions. It is in these realms that the sons of God are called not merely to visit but to inhabit and administer these higher dimensions.

THE THIRD HEBREW WORD IS SALAK סלק.

Salak סלק means **'to go up and ascend'**- but its deeper mystical significance points to a spiritual metamorphosis, a conscious evolution of the soul through dimensions of understanding. This ascension is consciousness expanding into our divine inheritance of governance.

Psalm 139:8 and Revelation 4:1 weave together a tapestry of divine invitation. When the psalmist declares, 'if I ascend to the heavens, you are there,' it speaks to the omnipresence of divinity, but also hints at humanity's latent ability to traverse celestial realms. This capability flowers fully in Revelation's imagery of the open door, not just an entry point, but a threshold between dimensions, beckoning the sons to step into the expanded realms of rulership.

The invitation to 'come up here' activates dormant spiritual capacities to unveil positional authority. The sons of God are called not to observe these higher dimensions, but to become active participants in their governance and administration. This participation creates a quantum entanglement between heavenly and earthly realms, where revelation knowledge flows between dimensions, becoming accessible keys for kingdom authority.

The maturation process in spiritual ascension is like the transformation of a caterpillar into a butterfly, each stage essential, each breakthrough expanding our capacity to hold and transmit divine light. This journey leads you into the mystery realms.

Examining John's ascension experience through the lens of the Greek text, we uncover layers of meaning that point to accessing what might be called spiritual DNA, the encoded memories of our governance in God. The Greek term for 'looked' (εἶδον/ eidon) means **'to possess knowledge and comprehend an activity'**. This connects to what ancient mystics called **'anamnesis',** the recollection of a primordial existence, allowing us to access insight carried in our spiritual structure from before time.

Acts 3:21 "Heaven must receive him until the time comes for God to restore everything, as he promised long ago through his holy prophets."

It speaks of the reactivation of divine blueprint, the remembrance of our original design and purpose in the heavenly realms. This restoration process involves awakening to multi-dimensional aspects of our being that have laid dormant, waiting for the proper time and spiritual maturity to be activated. This restoration is presented as a fulfilment of prophetic promises, indicating a return to an intended order and harmony that God originally planned.

The journey of סלק, then, becomes a sacred spiral of remembrance and reclamation, where each realm brings us closer to embodying our full divine potential. Through this process, we become living bridges between heaven and earth, channels through which divine governance can flow more fully into manifest reality.

'We ascend to unlock the forgotten treasures of our preexistence in Him', becomes more than a poetic statement - it's a key to understanding our role in the divine restoration of all things, where heaven and earth merge in a new expression of divine reality, a new creation.

GEMATRIA BREAKDOWN

Let's take a look at the gematria (numerical value) breakdown of the three ascension words as worlds:

1. ' - הללLah 'which represents level one of ascension.

Gematria = 5 ה, 30 ל

= 35 = 8 = ח **Chet**

2. ' - נשׂאNasa', representing level two.

Gematria = 1 א, 300 שׁ, 50 נ

= 351 = 9 = ט **Tet**

3. ' - קלסSalak', representing level three, the final phase.

Gematria = 100 ק, 30 ל, 60 ס

= 190 = 10 = י **Yod**

Mystical writings reveal that 'when the Holy One was about to create the world, all the letters of the alphabet were still hidden away. For two thousand years before the creation of the world, the Holy One, blessed be He, contemplated them and played with them. Each letter approached Him in turn, offering itself as the vehicle through which the world might be created.' In this way, each letter was imbued with divine wisdom, each containing hidden mysteries and energies that would later unfold in creation.

In this mystical unfolding, each Hebrew letter has a sacred numerical value known as gematria. As you delve into the depths of this ancient practice, the hidden staircase of ascension unfolds. Through the numerical values assigned to each word, a gradual progression unfolds, leading to the revelation of ascension.

Each ascension word represents a progression in maturity.

ח

The numerical value of the first ascension word corresponds to ח (Chet), the 8th letter in the Hebrew alphabet. Its literal meaning is **'to surround as a fence '**- a mystical enclosure that both protects and defines sacred space. In Hebrew, the word Chokmah חכמה begins with ח, meaning 'wisdom'. It represents the living, breathing wisdom that flows from the highest realms of divine insight.

Proverbs 8:22-23 "The LORD brought me forth as the first of his works, before his deeds of old; I was formed long ages ago, at the very beginning, when the world came to be." (Speaking of Wisdom/Chokmah)

Wisdom plays a crucial role in the process of unveiling ascension, serving as the initial infusion of revelation and the awakening of identity. Wisdom illuminates what was always present but hidden from conscious awareness. She descends like dew from the supernal realms, seeping into the spirit's deepest chambers, awakening identity.

Sirach (Ecclesiasticus) 24:3-7 "I came forth from the mouth of the Most High, and covered the earth like a mist. I dwelt in high places, and my throne was in a pillar of cloud."

It is within this realm that gates align and open to quicken purpose and destiny. These gates, spoken of in ancient texts as sha'arei tzedek (gates of righteousness). Each gate represents a threshold of consciousness, a doorway to adventure. This is the revealing of primordial existence, not just understanding it intellectually, but experiencing the resonance of creation's first moments still echoing through reality. It is the recognition of your position in the kingdom, where every son has its unique frequency and purpose. The call to ascend your mountain is not merely metaphorical, it is an invitation to climb the inner heights of consciousness, to stand where heaven and earth meet, where the finite touches the infinite.

Like Moses ascending Sinai, this climbing of your spiritual mountain represents your spirit's journey to its realm of revelation and transformation. Each step upward aligns more closely with the divine blueprint encoded in your being, activating ancient promises and prophecies written in the scroll of your destiny.

ט

The numerical value of the second ascension word ends with 9, symbolised by ט (Tet), the 9th letter in the Hebrew alphabet, which translates to **'basket'** or **'womb.'** This letter serves as a glory carrier, a cosmic cradle where consciousness enters the divine trans-dance. Like a mystical container woven from light, it holds the essence of our metamorphosis, echoing the sacred architecture of creation.

In this realm, we engage in the threefold trans-dance: **trans-relocation**, moving beyond spatial constraints into realms where distance dissolves into pure presence, where every point contains the whole, and consciousness flows like liquid light through the membranes between dimensions. Here, movement becomes intention, and intention becomes reality.

The second aspect, **transformation**, manifests as the alchemical reshaping of our spiritual DNA into increasingly refined light bodies. Our blueprint is rewritten in the language of heaven, each cellular memory transcoded into pure light information, dancing with the quantum pulse of your destiny.

The **Zohar** describes the symbolism of the Hebrew letter ט Tet:

"The ninth letter, Tet, is concealed and surrounded on all sides, like a woman who is pregnant. It is hidden and does not reveal its light outwardly, yet it is called 'good' because it contains a hidden light within it. This is the goodness that is concealed, waiting to emerge and bring forth light. The shape of the letter encloses the light, like a womb, nurturing the hidden essence that will one day be revealed. Thus, ט symbolises the hidden goodness that resides within creation, emerging at the appointed time."

Finally, **transfiguration** emerges, where our essence is illuminated from within, radiating divine light as Moses did upon Mount Sinai. This state transcends mere luminescence; it is a fundamental shift in the very nature of our being. We become living portals of divine expression, our bodies transformed into translucent vessels of infinite light, each atom singing in harmony with the cosmic chorus. Like prisms of consciousness, we refract the pure white light of divinity into rainbow bridges between worlds.

This triad of transcendent movement forms an eternal spiral dance in ascendance, each cycle lifting us higher through the dimensions of being. In this sacred geometry of movement, we become both dancers and the dance, observers and the observed, unified in the eternal moment of becoming.

ı

The third ascension word's numerical value concludes with י (Yod), the 10th letter of the Hebrew alphabet, representing the fulfilment of creation from its birth. This Yod, as the smallest letter, contains within it the paradox of completion - the ending returns to a new beginning, like a seed holding infinite potential. The three essential words reveal the process of how Yahweh is maturing you, expanding your spirit in concentric circles of awareness, like ripples spreading across the waters of consciousness.

To paraphrase the **Zohar** "When the Will of the Infinite arose to bring forth creation, it did so by emanating a hidden and concealed light. This light was veiled within itself, not yet revealed, until it began to expand and form pathways for the flow of life to the worlds. From this concealed light came a spark, a supernal point, which became the foundation of all that was to be. This point expanded and spread, forming channels and structures through which divine energy could descend. The process unfolded in silence, for none could comprehend the depths of this hidden wisdom, which sustains all realms."

Your consciousness is being carefully stretched and reshaped, like a vessel being widened to hold more light, so you can operate from the realm of completion - the place where heaven and earth meet within your own being.

The **Zohar** continues to expand "The point [of creation] when it first emerged was of an exceeding fineness, a locked secret, comprehended in a pure and tenuous thought. This point was hidden within the infinite light, and it emerged as the foundation of all things. When this point expanded, what remained of it became a palace for the divine, a holy place where the hidden could dwell. When this palace was completed, it served as a seed for all creation, a source from which all worlds would sprout. This palace holds within it the mysteries of the beginning, a vessel for the divine light that flows into all existence."

This expanded state allows you to perceive reality through multiple dimensions simultaneously, seeing different spiritual aspects of creation as one unified whole. Jesus wants to show you everything, not just surface understanding, but the intricate patterns that weave through all the heavens, the sacred geometries that underlie the spirit realm, the divine presence permeating every particle of creation. This 'everything' encompasses both the manifest and non manifest realms, the seen and unseen, the known and the mysterious unknown, that lie waiting to be revealed.

In the **Sefer Yetzirah** "Ten Sefirot of Nothingness: Their measure is ten which have no end. A depth of beginning, a depth of no end...»

Within the mystical architecture of the Hebrew letters, we uncover a sacred staircase of consciousness that is illuminated by three essential letters: Chet (ח), Tet (ט), and Yod ('). Together, they form a progressive journey of spiritual elevation. Chet (ח), being the eighth letter, establishes the foundation through wisdom (Chokmah). Like a sacred fence, it creates a protected space where divine revelation can unfold. Within this space, the gates of righteousness open, marking the threshold where one's unique spiritual frequency awakens to its divine purpose. As we ascend to Tet (ט), the ninth letter, we enter a transformative vessel, a cosmic womb, where consciousness undergoes a threefold metamorphosis. Through trans-relocation, transformation, and transfiguration, the soul becomes a living prism of divine light, transcending dimensional boundaries and merging with the eternal dance of creation. Finally, in Yod ('), the tenth letter, we encounter the paradox of completion that initiates new beginnings. Though physically the smallest letter, it represents the fullness of divine potential, where expanded consciousness perceives multiple dimensions simultaneously. Here, the merging of heaven and earth are quickened within the spirit, unveiling the intricate patterns of creation in both revealed and hidden realms. This sequence of ascension reveals a profound process of spiritual maturation, where each letter builds upon the previous, creating an ever-expanding spiral of consciousness that unveils divine unity and the oneness we have in Yahweh.

MOSES, THE ASCENSION LADDER

Moses stands as the archetypal prophet in Jewish and Christian faith, a foundational figure embodying the intersection of divine revelation and human leadership and administration.

Deuteronomy 34:10-12 "Since then, no prophet has risen in Israel like Moses, whom the LORD knew face to face...»

Born into the Levite tribe during a time of Hebrew enslavement in Egypt, his very survival was miraculous and orchestrated by God. His mother, Jochebed, facing Pharaoh's decree to kill Hebrew male infants, placed him in a papyrus basket on the Nile. This act of desperate faith led to his rescue by Pharaoh's daughter, who named him Moses ("drawn from water") and raised him in the Egyptian royal court.

This dual identity, raised as Egyptian royalty while being Hebrew by birth, shaped Moses's unique and mystical destiny. His formative years provided him with an education in Egyptian wisdom and leadership, while maintaining a deep connection to his Hebrew roots through his birth family, particularly his siblings Aaron and Miriam, who would later play crucial roles in the Exodus narrative.

The turning point came when Moses, witnessing an Egyptian taskmaster beating a Hebrew slave, killed the Egyptian and had to flee to Midian. This exile period proved crucial for his spiritual development. Under the mentorship of Jethro, a Midianite priest whose daughter Zipporah he married, Moses deepened his contemplative nature while working as a shepherd.

His profound encounter with God at the burning bush on Mount Horeb marked his transformation from shepherd to a pioneer in the mystic realms. This theophany introduced the ineffable divine name YHWH and started Moses's role as liberator and lawgiver. Jewish mystical tradition particularly emphasises this moment, seeing in the unconsumed burning bush both divine immanence and transcendence.

Moses's subsequent leadership encompassed multiple dimensions: miracle worker during the ten plagues, military leader during the Exodus, judge in tribal disputes, and most importantly, prophet and transmitter of divine law. His ascent of Mount Sinai for forty days and nights represents the peak of a mystical experience.

The **Zohar** describes this as entering the "cloud of unknowing," where Moses achieved the highest possible human communion with Yahweh.

Ecclesiasticus (Sirach) 45:1-5 "Beloved of God and men was Moses, whose memory is held in benediction. He made him equal in glory to the holy ones, and magnified him in the fears of his enemies... He sanctified him in his faithfulness and meekness, and chose him out of all flesh. He made him to hear his voice, and brought him into the dark cloud, and gave him commandments before his face, even the law of life and knowledge."

Traditional sources emphasise Moses's unique prophetic status: while other prophets received divine communication through dreams or visions, Moses spoke with God "face to face," with clear prophecy rather than riddles. Paradoxically, he could only see God's "back," not "face" when he asked to see God's glory. This encounter underscores both intimacy and the mystery of divine entanglement.

Numbers 12:6-8 "When there is a prophet among you, I, the LORD, reveal myself to them in visions, I speak to them in dreams. But this is not true of my servant Moses; he is faithful in all my house. With him I speak face to face, clearly and not in riddles; he sees the form of the LORD."

Despite leading the Israelites for forty years through the wilderness, Moses himself never entered the Promised Land, dying atop Mount Nebo within sight of it. Moses is a man who appeared to be insecure, stuttering in speech and likely lacking in confidence. When God first called him, his tongue was heavy with doubt and his spirit weighed down by his perceived limitations. He doubted himself deeply, and in his uncertainty requested that Aaron speak on his behalf. The enormity of his divine mission seemed greater than his faith in Yahweh's desire to act through him.

Initially, God sent Aaron as a bridge, a voice for the voiceless. As time unfurled its mysteries, Aaron stepped back into the shadows, watching in wonder as his brother's transformation unfolded. Moses' confidence grew through his extraordinary encounters with the heavenly realms on the mountain. The burning bush was merely the beginning. Each ascension into higher spiritual dimensions reshaped his nature, trumpeting the authority of his mountain, his destiny.

The realms he engaged with didn't merely influence Moses' confidence, they reconstructed his understanding of spiritual reality itself. With each divine encounter, each parting of the veils between worlds, his spiritual DNA seemed to shift and realign. Engaging with celestial domains expanded his consciousness. His words became revelations that shook both heaven and earth, his intercessions carrying the weight of one who had walked between worlds.

Talmud, *Rosh Hashanah* "Fifty gates of understanding (Binah) were created in the world, and all were given to Moses except one, as it is written: 'And You have made him a little lower than God' (Psalms 8:5)."

Walking through the worlds of the heavens, he trans-mutated from a place of believing into becoming. This wasn't just intellectual understanding - it was a divine manifestation that came from witnessing the machinery of creation. He had seen the framework that held reality together, had touched the building blocks of existence in the spirit realm. This knowing transformed him from a hesitant shepherd into a spiritual architect who could shape reality.

Wisdom of Sirach (Ecclesiasticus) 45:1-5 "Moses was beloved of God and men... He made him equal in glory to the holy ones, and made him great, to the terror of his enemies... He sanctified him in his faithfulness and meekness, and chose him out of all men."

Paraphrased from the **Zohar** "When Moses ascended to the heavens to receive the Torah, all the celestial beings trembled and said, 'What is one born of woman doing among us' The Holy One, blessed be He, responded to them, 'This is the one chosen to bring My light to the lower worlds.' Moses, elevated above the ordinary limitations of human flesh, became filled with the divine radiance, crowned with the glory of the Holy One. In that moment, he transcended the boundaries of earthly existence, standing as an equal among the higher beings. Through his spiritual ascent, Moses reached a level where his soul was united with the supernal light, enabling him to serve as a bridge between the heavens and the earth."

"Within the realms of ascension, confidence is born from encounters with heavenly dimensions that harmonise with your scroll aligned with destiny."

THE MYSTIC NAME OF MOSES

The name of Moses - משה Moshe in Hebrew - encodes the essence of the ascension experience:

- Mem (מ) symbolises water and represents the multidimensionality of the mysteries of the heavens. It signifies the unity of both male and female energies, hidden and revealed, coming together for the unfolding of divine creation.

- Shin (ש): represents fire, symbolising its purifying and transformative realm. The fire's glow, rising from the depths to the heavens, embodies the universe consuming all separation.

- Hey (ה): Denotes breath, showing face to face, a mouth פ

into mouth experience, intimate communion with Yahweh.

Moses' name embodied his ascension experience. He ascended into the waters, encountered the divine presence in fire, and spoke with God face-to-face, breath into breath entanglement. The mystery of his ascension journey remained hidden within his name, encoded in his DNA and expressed in his devotion to Yahweh.

Exodus 19:1-25 NIV "On the first day of the third month after the Israelites left Egypt—on that very day—they came to the Desert of Sinai.

2 After they set out from Rephidim, they entered the Desert of Sinai, and Israel camped there in the desert in front of the mountain.

3 Then Moses went up to God, and the Lord called to him from the mountain and said, "This is what you are to say to the descendants of Jacob and what you are to tell the people of Israel:

4 'You yourselves have seen what I did to Egypt, and how I carried you on eagles' wings and brought you to myself.

5 Now, if you obey me fully and keep my covenant, then out of all nations, you will be my treasured possession. Although the whole earth is mine,

6 you will be for me a kingdom of priests and a holy nation.' These are the words you are to speak to the Israelites."

7 So Moses went back and summoned the elders of the people and set before them all the words the Lord had commanded him to speak.

8 The people all responded together, "We will do everything the Lord has said." So Moses brought their answer back to the Lord.

9 The Lord said to Moses, "I am going to come to you in a

dense cloud, so that the people will hear me speaking with you and will always put their trust in you." Then Moses told the Lord what the people had said.

10 And the Lord said to Moses, "Go to the people and consecrate them today and tomorrow." Have them wash their clothes.

11 and be ready by the third day, because on that day the Lord will come down on Mount Sinai in the sight of all the people.

12 Put limits for the people around the mountain and tell them, 'Be careful that you do not approach the mountain or touch the foot of it. Whoever touches the mountain is to be put to death.

13 They are to be stoned or shot with arrows; not a hand is to be laid on them. No person or animal shall be permitted to live. " Only when the ram's horn sounds a long blast may they approach the mountain."

14 After Moses had gone down the mountain to the people, he consecrated them, and they washed their clothes.

15 Then he said to the people, "Prepare yourselves for the third day. Abstain from sexual relations."

16 On the morning of the third day there was thunder and lightning, with a thick cloud over the mountain, and a very loud trumpet blast. Everyone in the camp trembled.

17 Then Moses led the people out of the camp to meet with God, and they stood at the foot of the mountain.

18 Mount Sinai was covered with smoke, because the Lord descended on it in fire. The smoke billowed up from it like smoke from a furnace, and the whole mountain trembled violently.

19 As the sound of the trumpet grew louder and louder, Moses

spoke and the voice of God answered him.

20 The Lord descended to the top of Mount Sinai and called Moses to the top of the mountain. So Moses went up.

21 and the Lord said to him, "Go down and warn the people so they do not force their way through to see the Lord and many of them perish.

22 Even the priests, who approach the Lord, must consecrate themselves, or the Lord will break out against them."

23 Moses said to the Lord, "The people cannot come up Mount Sinai, because you yourself warned us, 'Put limits around the mountain and set it apart as holy.'"

24 The Lord replied, "Go down and bring Aaron up with you. But the priests and the people must not force their way through to come up to the Lord, or he will break out against them."

25 So Moses went down to the people and told them."

MULTI DIMENSIONAL GARMENTS

Exodus 19:1 On the first day of the third month after the Israelites left Egypt—on that very day—they came to the **Desert** of Sinai.

The Hebrew word for 'desert מִדְבַּר ,' (miḏ·bār), means **'barrenness or wilderness'**, but it also holds a hidden meaning,

'mouth'. Song of Solomon 5:15 describes the King's mouth as a source of exquisite sweetness. As the Israelites embarked on their journey, reaching the desert mountain meant more than just a physical arrival at a mountain; it signified their arrival at the mouth of the mountain, and perhaps even at the mouth of the King.

Yahweh's frequency is released from the mouth. The mouth is a source to breath, sound, frequency and vibration. Even though the Israelites reach a physical destination, they stepped into a spiritual reality.

The Hebrew root for מִדְבָּר is מַד, which means 'garment'. A derivative of מַד is מדד, which means 'to measure'. This suggests that garments serve as actual 'measures 'or 'calibrations 'of dimensional frequency.

From the Zohar "Each day, the soul is clothed in different garments, ascending and descending according to its deeds. These garments are woven from the actions and intentions of a person, and they determine the soul's journey and connection to the upper worlds. As the soul ascends, it wears garments of light and holiness;... These garments are the secret of the divine names, for through each garment, the soul connects to a specific name of the Holy One, blessed be He, reflecting the divine attributes in which the soul partakes." Another version describes it this way:

"When the soul comes into this world, it is covered with the garment of this world. This garment is of a lower realm, a garment of materiality that conceals the inner light of the soul. But through actions in this world, the soul can be elevated, transforming and purifying its garment. In this process, the soul gathers sparks of holiness scattered throughout creation, elevating them back to their divine source. When the soul departs from this world, it sheds this garment, purified and luminous, ascending to unite with the supernal realms."

מַד reveals a deeper spiritual principle about authority and dimensional transportation. In Hebrew mystical thought, garments aren't merely physical coverings, but represent spiritual technologies that enable transitional shifts between realms. These ascension garments function as vibrational interfaces that allow the spirit to harmonise with and access different dimensional frequencies.

There's a yearning in your spirit to be clothed...now...not when you die.

2 Corinthians 5:2-4 "Meanwhile we groan, longing to be clothed instead with our heavenly dwelling... For while we are in this tent, we groan and are burdened, because we do not wish to be unclothed but to be clothed instead with our heavenly dwelling"

This concept is illustrated in **2 Enoch 22:8**, which provides a description of dimensional transfiguration in ancient mystical literature:

'And the Lord said to Michael, "Go, and extract Enoch from |his| earthly clothing. And anoint him with my delightful oil, and put him into the clothes of my glory." And so Michael did, just as the Lord had said to him. He anointed me and he clothed me. And the appearance of that oil is greater than the greatest light, and its ointment is like sweet dew, and its fragrance myrrh; and it is like the rays of the glittering sun. And I looked at myself, and I had become like one of his glorious ones, and there was no observable difference.'

This passage reveals several key insights about ascension garments:

1. The process of exchange - removal of earthly/lower dimensional frequencies. There's a deliberate removal of "earthly clothing" before receiving higher dimensional

garments, suggesting distinct vibrational frequencies struggle to coexist simultaneously.

2. The role of anointing - anointing with divine light-substance. The mysterious oil serves as a transformational agent, described in terms of light, dew, and solar radiance - suggesting it affects multiple spiritual senses simultaneously. Frequency aligns you, fragrance ascends you.

3. Complete transformation into a higher dimensional state-clothing with garments of glory. Enoch's statement that there was "no observable difference" between himself and the glorious one shows these garments facilitate complete dimensional integration.

The process mirrors what Colossians 3:9-10 references regarding dimensional shifting - a putting off of the old nature and putting on of the new. These garments of light or glory represent different vibrational frequencies that allow consciousness to operate in various dimensional planes.

In mystical understanding, these garments serve several purposes:

- Frequency modulators for dimensional transit, act as interfaces between different levels of reality
- Carry specific authority markers that function in different realms
- Enable perception and operation in higher frequencies
- Facilitate communication between beings of different dimensional origins
- Technologies for perception and interaction in various spiritual dimensions

In the deeper mystical understanding, these garments represent graduated levels of consciousness and spiritual capacity that the sons mature into. Each garment corresponds to specific abilities to perceive and operate within different dimensional frequencies. The exchange of garments described isn't just symbolic - it represents actual changes in spiritual composition and capabilities. In simpler terms, spiritual garments are technologies that unlock and reveal the abilities inherent in you as an Elohim, a son of God.

1 Enoch 62:15-16 "And the righteous and elect shall have risen from the earth, And ceased to be of downcast countenance. And they shall have been clothed with garments of glory, And these shall be the garments of life from the Lord of Spirits."

3 Enoch 12:1-5 describes Metatron's transformation: "When the Holy One, blessed be he, took me from among those who walk on earth... He appointed me over all the treasuries and storehouses... He clothed me in a garment of glory."

Though the above scriptures are not about Moses, they are examples that tie in with his transformational process in ascension.

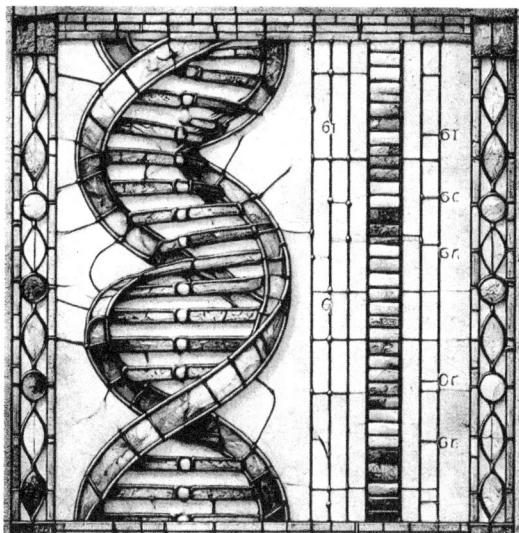

THE MEASURING, A HEALING JOURNEY

On the word מדד meaning **'to be measured'**. It reminds me of the movie 'A Knight's Tale', where the jousting opponent says, "You've been weighed, you've been measured, and you've been found wanting." And there's a scripture for that: **Daniel 5:27**

"TEKEL: You have been weighed on the scales and found wanting"

Psalm 139:23-24 "Search me, God, and know my heart; test me and know my anxious thoughts. See if there is any offensive way in me...»

During your spiritual journey, you will traverse through the essential valley of self-reflection and pruning, the measuring phase. This period of introspection is where transformation begins. Jesus, in His infinite wisdom and compassion, stands as both guide and healer, helping illuminate the shadowed corners of your soul where past hurts, deep-seated trauma, and unresolved disappointments are.

This divine partnership in healing isn't just about mending old wounds, it's about reconstructing your spiritual DNA as a son of God. Like a master artisan carefully restoring a priceless artifact, each piece of emotional healing adds depth, richness, and authority to your spirituality. Think of it as spiritual archaeology - each layer of healing uncovers new dimensions of your divine inheritance and authority.

The correlation between healing and spiritual authority is multifaceted. As you heal, your spiritual awareness grows, giving you a wider perspective and greater wisdom to manage life's difficulties. These challenges offer carefully orchestrated opportunities for spiritual refinement and elevation. Each trial becomes a doorway to deeper understanding and greater authority when approached from a place of emotional wholeness.

Your journey will demand consistency, which requires you to shed old paradigms. This metamorphosis affects everything: how you pray, how you lead, how you love, how you serve. The authority to govern and make kingdom decisions flows naturally from a healed heart.

Consider this: attempting to exercise spiritual authority while carrying unhealed wounds is like trying to conduct an orchestra with broken arms. The music of your life becomes discordant, your decisions clouded by unresolved pain. The weight of emotional wounds creates distortions in your spiritual lens, leading to decisions that stem from hurt rather than wisdom, from fear rather than faith.

I've witnessed countless individuals blessed with extraordinary spiritual gifts and powerful anointing, yet they often quit not because of a lack of calling, but because of emotional immaturity. Their attempt at building ministries, though bright, burn out or quit, and traces back to unhealed wounds and unprocessed trauma. Inner healing gives you fresh eyes, so situations that once defeated you become opportunities for victory. The same trials that once drained you become wellsprings of wisdom. This is the sustainable transformation that true healing brings.

2 Corinthians 3:18 Mirror Bible "The days of window-shopping are over! In him every face is unveiled. In gazing with wonder at the blueprint of God displayed in human form, we suddenly realise that we are looking into a mirror, where every feature of his image articulated in Christ is reflected within us! The Spirit of the Lord engineers this radical transformation; we are led from an inferior mind-set to the revealed endorsement of our authentic identity."

Remember: healing isn't about feeling better - it's about becoming you, the original you. It's about maturing into the fullness of your divine calling. Each step in your healing journey is a step toward promotion in the spiritual realm. As your heart heals, your authority expands, your wisdom deepens, and your ministry or journey becomes powerful and sustainable. When internal healing aligns with external anointing, that's when lasting impact occurs. That's when transformation becomes not only personal, but generational.

Healing, therefore, doesn't just lead to promotion - it is the very base on which lasting spiritual authority is built. It's the bridge between potential and manifestation, between calling and fulfilment, between gifting and legacy.

THE AWAKENING

As the Israelites ventured into the desert and approached the mountain, unbeknownst to them, they found themselves in a spiritual reality, coming face to face with the voice of Yahweh.

Moses, in particular, had a close entanglement with Yahweh, speaking to Him face to face. The Hebrew word for 'face' is פָּנִים 'panim' and is linked to פה Pey פ, meaning 'mouth', so Moses had an intimate interaction with Yahweh.

Numbers 12:8 "With him I speak face to face (פה אל-פה,

peh el peh), clearly and not in riddles; he sees the form of the LORD."

The Hebrew implies it was not just a face-to-face interaction, but a mouth into mouth, a divine breath entangling breath. Yahweh brought the Israelites to a location where they could tangibly encounter His frequency and breath.

In this place, a profound awakening of consciousness occurs as the face, mouth, and breath of Yahweh play a crucial role in the initial stage of ascending and experiencing divine encounters on your mountain.

As the Israelites reached the base (discussed later) of Mount Sinai, the realm of the mouth, a spiritual awakening began to stir within them. Interestingly, both Sinai סִינַי as well as ascension סלק start with Samech ס , which is the Hebrew letter that surrounds.

They entered the gateway to primordial creation, a space where they could connect with the original purpose of their existence.

The Hebrew word for Sinai סִינַי, is significant in the context of this quickening. The specific root meaning of Sinai is uncertain, but there is speculation it comes from the root word סנה 'Seneh', meaning 'bush', as in the burning bush. This connection relates to Moses 'first encounter with God at the burning bush.

From the **Zohar** "When the Holy One, blessed be He, called to Moses from the burning bush, that call resonated and penetrated all the firmaments, reaching the upper worlds and the lower worlds alike. All the heavenly hosts trembled and listened, and the divine voice traveled through all realms. In that moment, Moses was crowned with the supernal crown of complete faith. The Holy One called him by name, 'Moses, Moses,' drawing him close, enveloping him in holiness, and bestowing upon him the authority of divine wisdom, for he was chosen to lead the children of Israel out of bondage and into light."

REALMS OF SPIRITUAL ENTITIES

In Exodus 3:1-6 NIV Now Moses was tending the flock of Jethro his father-in-law, the priest of Midian, and he led the flock to the far side of the wilderness and came to Horeb, **the mountain of God**. There the angel of the Lord appeared to him in flames of fire from within a bush. Moses saw that though the bush was on fire it did not burn up. So Moses thought, "I will go over and see this strange sight—why the bush does not burn up." When the Lord saw that he had gone over to look, God called to him from within the bush, "Moses! Moses!" And Moses said, "Here I am." "Do not come any closer," God said. "Take off your sandals, for the place where you are standing is holy ground." Then he said, "I am the God of your father, the God of Abraham, the God of Isaac and the God of Jacob." At this, Moses hid his face, because he was afraid to look at God.'

Horeb, the mountain of God, presents a profound theological complexity through its use of Elohim (אלהים) as God. Traditional Christianity will narrow down Elohim to Father, Son and Holy Spirit. However, this plural form of divinity suggests a celestial court or divine council. The mountain itself serves as a structure where divine authority manifests in multiple thrones.

Daniel 7:9 NIV provides a vivid portrayal: "thrones were set in place and the Ancient of Days took his seat. His clothing was white as snow, his hair white like wool. His throne was flaming with fire and its wheels were all ablaze."

This scene depicts not just a single throne, but multiple seats of authority, suggesting a divine assembly or celestial court. The Ancient of Days, presented in glory, presides over this gathering of celestial authorities.

This hierarchical arrangement finds parallel confirmation in **Revelation 4:2 NIV** "At once I was in the spirit, and there before me was a throne in heaven with someone sitting on it. And the one who sat had the appearance of Jasper and Ruby. A rainbow that shone like an emerald encircled and surrounding the throne, with 24 other thrones, and seated on them the 24 elders."

The imagery of thrones creates a cosmic amphitheater of divine governance.

When Moses approached Mount Horeb, he was essentially entering a celestial court in session. The burning bush encounter can be understood as stepping into a divine council where celestial beings occupied their respective thrones. These divine beings, having taken part in heavenly deliberations, were prepared for Moses's arrival and their role in conveying divine instruction.

A passage from the **Zohar** reveals "At the time when Moses ascended on high, all the heavenly hosts trembled and said: 'What is one born of woman doing among us?' ... And when they saw the cloud that raised Moses and he entered among them...»

The burning bush itself served as a portal or gateway into this realm of divine assembly. The angel of the Lord manifesting in the fire represents an interplay between divine messenger and divine presence. The seraphim (שרפים, literally "burning ones") created an atmosphere of sanctified space through their fiery presence. These beings of living flame, each carrying specific divine mandates, created a multidimensional spiritual environment.

This understanding becomes particularly significant in contemplating spiritual ascension practices. The angels of fire, positioned at the mountain's base where "measuring" occurs, suggest a transformation point - a threshold where human consciousness must be calibrated or "measured" before ascending further into divine realms.

In **Psalm 82:1 NIV** "God presides in the great assembly; he renders judgment among the 'gods'" - reinforcing the concept of divine council meetings.

1 Kings 22:19 NIV adds: "I saw the Lord sitting on his throne with all the multitudes of heaven standing around him on his right and on his left."

These references collectively paint a picture of elaborately structured spiritual realms, where divine authority operates through multiple levels and beings, all ultimately serving Yahweh's supreme authority.

In **Isaiah 6:1**, it is described how the prophet saw the Lord seated on a throne, surrounded by seraphim with six wings each. These entities covered their faces and feet with two wings and flew with the other two.

Acts 7:38 NIV - 'He was in the assembly in the wilderness, with the angel who spoke to him on mount Sinai, and with our ancestors; and he received living words to pass on to us.'

Both **Psalm 82:1** and **Acts 7:38** mention the 'assembly'. The Hebrew word for this 'assembly 'is 'SOD סוד ', which means **'to receive counsel from Yahweh in the mysteries of heaven.'** This divine council, this celestial gathering, represents a convergence point between the earthly and heavenly realms. Imagine being in the midst of that! The very atmosphere is charged with divine mysteries. Surely this is where Moses found himself at the burning bush.

Interacting with spiritual entities on the mountain of God - is essential during ascension practice and serves as a key to unlock consciousness. Our focus remains steadfast on the divine trio of Yahweh, Jesus, and the Holy Spirit. Yet, it is also a time of profound connection with our spiritual family, who emanate God's presence.

You want to encounter angels, to engage in divine dialogue as Daniel did in

Daniel 10:15 'When he had spoken to me according to these words, I turned my face toward the ground and was dumb. 16 And behold, one in the likeness of the sons of men touched my lips. Then I opened my mouth and spoke. I said to him who stood before me, O my lord, by reason of the vision sorrows and pains have come upon me, and I retain no strength.'

His desire is that we communicate with them and hear their response, much like the prophets of old who conversed with heavenly messengers.

This section aims to activate your interaction with spiritual beings, as described in scriptures. Our journey surpasses the confines of emotions but the spiritual ecstasy though these are indeed wonderful manifestations, and I love to engage them. It involves opening our gates because scripture declares in **1 Corinthians 6:3** that as sons, we will judge the angels. This empowers us to exercise our authority in spiritual affairs. If we lack comprehension of the details and the keys needed for activation, how can we possibly judge the situation? While the Christian faith traditionally holds that judging the angels and ascension occur after our earthly life, this perspective might require a fresh look. With Jesus' ascension and the cosmic victory of the cross already accomplished, we are now positioned to experience this reality, because death is no longer our gateway. As **Colossians 3:1** declares, since we are risen with Christ, we seek those things which are above. Through the power of Jesus within, we are understanding and navigate the process of spiritual ascension.

Our relationship with Jesus is deepening, and we are being given mandates and authority, much like the authority given to Adam in Genesis to steward creation. Yahweh has given us power to govern creation, as outlined in

Genesis 1:26-28 NIV Then God said, "Let us make mankind in our image, in our likeness, so that they may rule over the fish in the sea and the birds in the sky, over the livestock and all the wild animals, and over all the creatures that move along the ground." So God created mankind in his own image, in the image of God he created them; male and female he created them. God blessed them and said to them, "Be fruitful and increase in number; fill the earth and subdue it. Rule over the fish in the sea and the birds in the sky and over every living creature that moves on the ground."

This sacred partnership holds the power to heal and align creation with its original design, as **Romans 8:19-22** speaks of creation yearning for the manifestation of God's sons. Like Elisha's servant, who saw the heavenly armies when his eyes were opened in **2 Kings 6:17**, ascension is revealing a new creation vision from heaven. As **Jeremiah 23:18** hints, that we have the potential to be part of the council. It enables us to join the "council of the holy ones," as described in **Psalm 89:7**, by sitting at the table and interacting with others present. This is such an exciting realm of sonship.

We can make it all about spiritual mysteries in the kingdom of heaven, but God also wants to reveal mysteries within your business, your workplace, your family. The mysteries from the kingdom are revealed, giving you unique insights and knowledge that transcend human understanding. These divine revelations can manifest in the most unexpected moments - during a routine meeting, at your desk, or even in the middle of a family dinner. It's Yahweh speaking through you, transforming the hidden into divine insight. Knowledge will come forth that you never studied, understanding will emerge that you never learned through conventional means. All because you entangle a divine council.

THE ENTERING

Exodus 19:2 NIV 'After they set out from Rephidim, they **entered** the Desert of Sinai, and Israel camped there in the desert in front of the mountain.'

The Hebrew word for 'entered' is בוא (bo), and reveals layers of profound spiritual significance that translations don't fully capture. בוא means to **'come or go'**.

John 10:9 NIV 'I am the gate; whoever enters through me

will be saved.⁰ They will come in and go out, and find pasture.'

This divine combination of letters tells a story of cosmic proportions:

Sefer Yetzirah 2:4 "Twenty-two foundation letters: He engraved them, He carved them, He permuted them, He weighed them, He transformed them, And He created with them everything that was created and everything that would be created."

"The Hebrew letters are DNA structures written in the language of heaven"

The ב (bet) represents not just any temple, but the living temple - the indwelling of divine presence in the sons of God. As the first letter of the Torah (בראשית / Bereshit), it speaks of the container that holds sacred space and the blueprints of all of creation. This temple aspect suggests that when Israel "entered", they weren't merely moving through physical space, but entering a dimensional gateway, the portal of creation's release.

Genesis 28:17 (Jacob's experience) - "How awesome is this place! This is none other than the house of God (בית אלהים / Beit Elohim), and this is the gate of heaven."

The ו (vav) as the DNA ladder or 'peg' connects heaven and earth, much like Jacob's vision at Bethel. The vav serves as a cosmic connector, joining dimensional realms, the channel through which the wonders flow.

The א (alef) culminates this trinity of letters with silent power. As the first letter of the Hebrew alphabet, it represents the ineffable nature of the divine - the realm beyond human comprehension. It is both nothing and everything, the paradox of manifest divinity, our arcing from the end into the beginning.

This connects powerfully to Moses's role with the staff and

wonders פלא pala. The reverse spelling of אלף alef in פלא suggests these wonders emerge from behind the veil of mystery, turning the ineffable into manifest reality. Moses, as the intermediary, could access these mysteries through the unveiling ascension of לה, becoming a living bridge between realms.

In the **Zohar** "When a person ascends to unite above, all the worlds rejoice with him, and the Holy One, blessed be He, calls all His hosts and says to them: 'See the precious son I have in the lower world!' When one unites below with holiness, causing joy in all worlds, his actions draw blessings and light to all realms. The Holy One takes pride in this soul, as it unites the lower with the upper worlds, bringing harmony and fulfilment to all creation."

This mirrors Jacob's profound experience, where his vision of angels ascending and descending wasn't merely a dream but a revelation of humanity's potential for divine connection. The angels ascending first from Jacob himself suggest that the divine spark originates within us, making each son of God a gateway to higher and inter-dimensional realms. As Jacob witnessed angels ascending first (then descending), it established a pattern: you are the chosen temple, the gateway of first release.

This mystical perspective suggests that the Israelites' entrance into the desert wasn't merely geographical - it was a dimensional shift into a space where heaven and earth meet, where the mysteries of the kingdom can be unlocked because of their presence as living temples of God.

2 Enoch 21:1-6 "And those men took me from there, and they brought me up to the seventh heaven... And I saw there an exceptionally great light, and all the fiery armies of the great archangels, and the incorporeal forces and the dominions and the origins and the authorities, the cherubim and the seraphim and the many-eyed thrones...»

The desert itself could symbolise a stripping away, creating the empty space necessary for divine revelation, and mirrors the Israelites 'journey from the physical (leaving Rephidim) to the mystical (entering Sinai's desert). The sequence of these letters in בוא is significant as the integration of temple consciousness (bet), transformational ascension (vav), and divine mystery (alef) creates a template for spiritual evolution that remains accessible through these Hebrew letters.

THE FOUR REALMS OF DIVINE ENCOUNTER

Exodus 19:3 NIV Then Moses **went up** to God. The Lord **called to** Moses from the mountain. He said, "This is what you should say to the descendants of Jacob and the people of Israel."

The phrase 'went up' is the first ascension word, לה, which we discussed earlier in the book.

The Lord 'called to' him from the mountain, using the Hebrew word qara 'קָרָא', which primarily means to **'summon, announce, invoke, and worship'**.

1. THE SUMMONS

The first realm began with Yahweh's call as he summoned him to enter His divine presence. This wasn't merely an invitation, but a fundamental restructuring of Moses's spiritual DNA, an alignment preparing him for the weight of glory he would encounter. This calling activated dormant spiritual frequencies within Moses's spirit, preparing him for the dimensional shift he was about to experience. The summons formed a quantum bridge, built from the very song of creation that Yahweh sang over Moses upon his release into existence.

Exodus 3:4 "When the LORD saw that he had gone over to look, God called to him from within the bush, 'Moses! Moses!' And Moses said, 'Here I am.'

This double calling of the name is significant in Hebrew mysticism, suggesting a calling to both lower and higher realms.

2. THE DIVINE POSITIONING

God made a public announcement, summoning Moses into the spirit realm. The Lord called him and declared him as a son entering the mountain.

Psalms 2:7 "I will proclaim the Lord's decree: He said to me, 'You are my son; today I have become your father.'

This proclamation resounded in both the visible and invisible realms, establishing Moses's authority across multiple dimensions. This announcement mirrored Moses's arrival in the divine's court, granting him cosmic authorisation to navigate spiritual territories.

Hebrews 12:22-24 "But you have come to Mount Zion, to the city of the living God, the heavenly Jerusalem. You have come to thousands upon thousands of angels in joyful assembly, to the church of the firstborn..."

3. THE INVOCATION OF DIVINE IDENTITY

The acknowledgment of Moses's nature as Elohim was not merely a symbolic title; it signified his empowered position. The designation of "sons of God" as Elohim (which Jesus later affirmed when confronted by the Pharisees) unveiled our divine lineage as reflectors of Yahweh's image. We belong to the tribe of Elohim. Yahweh summoned forth Moses's divine standing, stirring the latent seeds of celestial ancestry within him.

Zohar (verified from the Vilna edition): "When it arose in the will of the Holy One, blessed be He, to create the world, He brought forth one flame from the lamp of severe judgment, and blew spirit upon spirit, and they were included one within the other, and He brought forth one image. And that image is the partnership of all, upper and lower, and this is Elohim."

The Zohar discusses the relationship between human beings and the name Elohim: "When a person performs the commandments of the Torah and walks in its ways, then they are called Elohim."

Exodus 7:1 "Then the LORD said to Moses, 'See, I have made you like God [Elohim] to Pharaoh'"

Psalm 82:6 "I said, 'You are gods [Elohim], and all of you are sons of the Most High'

John 10:34-36 "Jesus answered them, 'Is it not written in your Law, 'I have said you are "gods"'? If he called them 'gods,' to whom the word of God came—and Scripture cannot be set aside—what about the one whom the Father set apart as his very own and sent into the world?'"

3 Enoch 4:1-2 "When the Holy One, blessed be he, took me from the generation of the flood, he lifted me on the wings of the winds of Shekinah to the highest heaven... He made me a throne similar to the throne of glory."

4. THE WORSHIP DIMENSION

The prostration before Yahweh represents more than physical genuflection - it's a complete alignment of one's multidimensional being with the divine frequency of His image. He is worthy of all. This form of worship creates a resonance field that allows for deeper penetration into the divine realms of reverence. From worship, into worship, to becoming worship.

To bring it together, the realms delve into the deep spiritual transformation of Moses, exploring four interconnected dimensions that all stem from the Hebrew word qara קָרָא. It all begins with the divine summons, which leads Moses to undergo a fundamental restructuring of his spiritual essence. This prepares him for a divine encounter filled with glory. This initial call creates a "quantum bridge," connecting Moses to his original divine purpose. From there, the summons seamlessly transitions into a public divine positioning, establishing Moses's authority across various spiritual realms. This proclamation serves as heaven's official recognition of his status, bridging the visible and invisible domains. This positioning opens the door to the next dimension: the invocation of divine identity. Through this, Moses's nature as Elohim is revealed, connecting him to a broader divine lineage and purpose. Finally, these three dimensions culminate in the worship dimension, where Moses's entire being aligns with divine frequencies, the sound of Yahweh. This final stage goes beyond physical prostration, representing a complete multidimensional resonance with a divine nature. It transforms Moses from someone who worships into an embodiment of worship itself.

THE MATRIX REVELATION (קרא TO קרב)

Here's an intriguing discovery. The word 'call קָרָא' means to 'encounter 'or 'meet'. Interestingly, when you replace the א (the wonders) in קרא with a ב (the temple manifestation of the wonders) to קרב, you get the word 'womb'... which also carries the meaning of 'matrix'. In this context, you are the ב (bet), the temple, the embodiment of the ascension matrix. The linguistic transformation from קרא (call/encounter/meet) to קרב (womb/matrix) reveals a beautiful mystical truth: The ascension experience is actually an entry into a spiritual womb, where birthing and transformation occurs. This matrix serves several functions:

- It serves as an incubation chamber for spiritual metamorphosis
- It functions as a download centre for divine revelation and wisdom
- It operates as a calibration zone where human consciousness can safely adjust to higher spiritual frequencies

This matrix realm represents the quantum field of divine possibility. When God called upon Moses to enter His divine presence, Moses found himself surrounded by the matrix of his divine purpose, his mountain. Within this sacred space, Moses fully immersed himself in the framed possibilities of his destiny. The transformation of קרא to קרב isn't just wordplay - it reveals how the act of responding to divine calling (קרא) transforms our being into a living temple (ב), capable of hosting and manifesting divine reality. This makes each ascension experience not just a personal elevation but a divine entanglement with spiritual heritage.

THE CHRIST PATTERN WITHIN

Yahweh's intention was to reveal to Moses timeless mysteries and what would come to pass when Jesus lived within the sons of God, the true temples. Moses would therefore experience something extraordinary, a sense of Christ within him, even before its outward revelation. This manifestation demonstrates a timeless blueprint for transformation. This pre-echo of Christ consciousness suggests that:

- Divine indwelling isn't limited by linear time.

John 8:58 "Before Abraham was, I am"

- The Christ pattern is embedded in the fabric of creation.

Colossians 1:15-17 "He is the image of the invisible God, the firstborn of all creation... He is before all things, and in him all things hold together."

Ascension experiences connect us to a timeless reality that goes beyond the limits of history, but into destiny.

Ecclesiastes 3:11 NIV 'He has made everything beautiful in its time. He has also set eternity in the human heart.'

"The matrix realm is the architecture of transformation, where the divine blueprint interfaces with human consciousness. In this space, past, present, and future converge, allowing access to timeless eternity."

The matrix acts as both a cradle for spiritual development and a springboard for dimensional travel. God summoned Moses into the matrix, the womb, and the inner chambers of his own mountain.

CONSTELLATION HOUSES OF GOVERNANCE

Exodus 19:3 NIV 'Then Moses went up **to** God. The LORD called **to** Moses from the mountain. He said,'

The Hebrew word for 'to 'is 'אל', also meaning **'into'**. The LORD called **'into'** Moses, activating his breath, entangling his being and igniting his purpose and destiny. This divine breath - the same creative force that spoke existence into being - penetrated the very essence of Moses 'consciousness, transforming him at the quantum level of spiritual reality. Moses had a face into face encounter with God as he went up INTO God.

Here, in the scripture, God is Elohim, divinity in plural form, a magnificent council of divine authority and power. Like entering a cosmic throne room of infinite dimensions, Moses ascended into the realm of the gods, the Elohim. The very atmosphere charged with divine presence, each breath drawing him deeper into celestial reality, where earthly physics held no dominion.

It was from this realm, likely in the councils, that Yahweh (the intimate covenant name of God), not Elohim, called out to him, establishing a personal covenant of intimacy. This shift from Elohim to Yahweh marks the transition from the councils to an intimate, personal encounter with the King Himself. Moses encountered the councils of gods and thrones on the mountain, where beings of light and power attended the eternal courts, but it was the King of Kings who summoned him, drawing him into an embrace of divine fellowship that would forever mark him as a man who knew God face to face. The mountain became more than a physical peak; it transformed Moses into a living gateway between realms, where divine councils convened and the breath of God shaped destinies.

Exodus 19:3 NIV

..."This is what you should say to the **descendants** of Jacob and the people of Israel."

Note the distinction between the descendants of Jacob and the people of Israel, as it holds great significance. In this ascension encounter, Moses's voice was activated. He came in from the mouth, entangling measuring and a new garment to having a new voice. Despite his previous struggles with speech, Yahweh activated Moses primordial sound. The Israelites were delivered and gathered in front of the mountain, but God specifically assigned Moses to address the descendants of Jacob, who were the fathers of the twelve tribes of Israel. The Hebrew word for "descendants" is "בַּיִת (bǎ·yiṯ)," which means 'temple,' emphasising their sacred connection to the constellation houses connected to realms of governance, storehouses and mysteries.

Rabbi Simeon in the Zohar said: 'When the Holy One, blessed be He, was about to create the world, He consulted with the souls of the righteous and with the celestial family above. He said, "Let us make humankind in our image, after our likeness" (Genesis 1:26). This consultation was with the celestial family and the souls of the righteous so that creation would be established with wisdom and counsel, in harmony with the upper and lower realms. By including the righteous souls, the world was formed with the qualities of mercy and justice, creating a foundation balanced between the heavens and the earth. Thus, humankind was made in the image of both realms, linking all creation together in divine harmony.'"

Job 38:31-33 "Can you bind the chains of the Pleiades? Can you loosen Orion's belt?... Do you know the laws of the heavens? Can you set up God's dominion over the earth?"

When God commanded Moses to speak, it was a profound spiritual entanglement with the descendants of Jacob, resulting in a physical manifestation over the people of Israel. He was speaking into the gate of creations release. The descendants embody them as sacred temples ב, the 12 tribes of Jacob, but also symbolising the matrix of the star systems. Each tribe represented a celestial sign intricately positioned within the spiritual plane of the Mazzaroth.

1 Enoch 72:1 "The book of the courses of the luminaries of the heavens, the relations of each, according to their classes, their dominion and their seasons...»

Moses found himself in the task of connecting with the temple houses of each tribal system in the spirit realm. His goal was to unlock the mandates and scrolls that contained the original intent of each tribe of Israel. It wasn't just a question of being descendants of Jacob, but a complete transition into becoming the people of Israel, a people of promised inheritance.

As God instructed Moses to speak, he realised his authority in the spiritual realm. God bestowed upon him the sceptre of kingship, enabling him to govern and release the destinies of the tribes to the people of Israel. It went beyond simply delivering a message; Moses had to embrace his role as a king and actively engage with the tribes in the spirit realm. Through this interaction, he would govern over them and unleash the unique gifts and purposes they carried for the people of Israel. The destiny that was encapsulated within the memory of the heavenly waters. This signifies the profound impact that occurs when we become entangled in the process of ascension.

Testament of Levi 8:2-3 "And I saw seven men in white clothing, who were saying to me: 'Arise, put on the robe of the priesthood, and the crown of righteousness, and the oracle of understanding...'"

God will reveal to you your role in governing the spirit realm. This may begin with small tasks or you may have already been engaged in it for some time. Your role can be significant, no matter the size or nature of it. The important thing is that Jesus is entrusting you with the responsibility of overseeing temples and thrones in the spirit realm as you ascend. Your purpose is to govern from those positions and fulfil your own calling. You hold positions in the heavenly realms, where the entire cosmos revolves around God's throne. You ascend and God places you over thrones to govern into the physical realm. Prayer is evolving, and relying solely on asking Jesus for everything is like speaking as a child. It won't suffice because Jesus wants you to embrace your position in the spirit realm as a son of God, as an Elohim. This may unsettle some, but it's time to move beyond the basics. Jesus has granted you authority, so establish laws and take action.

"Jesus has entrusted you with the responsibility of governing the spirit realm, regardless of the size or nature of your role. Embrace your position as a son of God and establish laws, for you hold positions in the heavenly realms that impact the physical realm. It is time to move beyond the basics and fulfil your calling with authority.

THE WATERS OF THE AGES

Exodus 19:9 NIV The Lord said to Moses, "I am **going to come** to you in a dense **cloud**, so that the people will hear me speaking with you and will always put their trust in you." Then Moses told the Lord what the people had said.

The Hebrew term used for 'going to come 'is once again 'bo' בוא to 'come and go', and 'to you 'is אל i.e into or inside of you.

This is not merely an external visitation, but an internal transformation where the infinite enters the finite. It represents a complete state of ecstasy, a divine entanglement. The dense cloud that Yahweh manifests within contains not just physical vapour, but carries within it the crystallised wisdom of the ages - each droplet suspended in perfect harmony, vibrating with the frequency of divine mysteries.

Zohar describes this passage "When Moses ascended into the cloud, it was not merely a physical cloud, but rather a garment of light, a cloak that allowed him to perceive the higher realms. This cloud served as a shield and a transformative state, enabling Moses to approach the divine fire and gaze upon the supernal mysteries. Through this garment of light, he transcended the limitations of earthly perception, entering a state of consciousness attuned to the divine. Wrapped in this cloud, Moses was able to draw near and receive wisdom that was beyond ordinary understanding."

Wisdom of Solomon 7:25-26 "For she is the breath of the power of God, and a pure influence flowing from the glory of the Almighty... For she is the brightness of the everlasting light, the unspotted mirror of the power of God."

The cloud serves as a metaphysical interface, a membrane between dimensions where the natural and supernatural converges. When Moses ascends and entangles with these celestial memories, he becomes a living conduit for supernatural revelation. The cloud becomes a portal of transformation, where each particle holds encoded wisdom waiting to be unlocked through divine communion. This sacred mist carries within it the DNA of creation itself - the building blocks of reality that respond to awakened consciousness.

1 Enoch 14:8-9 "And behold I saw the clouds: And they were calling me in a vision; and the fogs were calling me; and the course of the stars and the lightnings were rushing me and causing me to desire."

The ascension process initiates a quantum leap in spiritual authority. As we rise into these higher dimensions of awareness, our capacity to operate in both spiritual and physical realms expands exponentially. Each encounter recalibrates our spiritual senses, allowing us to perceive and interact with reality. The memory of water within the cloud becomes a living library of cosmic wisdom, accessible through states of heightened consciousness.

Yahweh orchestrated this demonstration not just for Moses's benefit, but to establish a pattern for all who would follow - showing that genuine spiritual ascension manifests tangible evidence in both seen and unseen realms. When consciousness expands into these divine dimensions, the experience may seem too extraordinary to be real, yet it is more real than our limited physical reality. This expanded state of being allows us to function, bringing forth heavenly realities into earthly situations.

The authority gained in spiritual realms becomes anchored in our being when we fully embrace and operate from this elevated consciousness. However, doubt and hesitation can create resistance in this process, causing our awareness to contract rather than expand. Creation itself resonates with and responds to awakened consciousness. It awaits the sons of God to operate from this place of knowing and authority.

This journey continuously unfolds new layers of revelation and transformation. As we engage with these mysteries, we are not only observing them - we are being metabolised by them, transformed into living expressions of divine reality. Each encounter reshapes our understanding and expands our capacity to manifest kingdom authority in every sphere of influence. It unlocks not just what we perceive, but alters who we are becoming, living gateways through which heaven's realities can flow into earth's experience.

2 Esdras 14:37-40 "Then was I as a fountain of understanding, of wisdom, and of knowledge... my heart uttered understanding, and wisdom grew in my breast, for my spirit strengthened my memory."

"Embrace the mysteries of the waters, for within them lies the power to unlock your true identity and co-create your reality. It unlocks what we look into, what we engage into, and what we are being transformed into."

When creation is unlocked, it responds to its original intent. Ascension allows us to engage with this unlocking process. Moses experienced this when he encountered the waters of the heavenly realms in the cloud of glory. These experiences revealed the original memory and intent of Yahweh's relationship with Moses. He brings you face to face with these primordial memories, unlocking truth.

Like Moses, who emerged from the cloud with his face radiating divine light, our inner being becomes increasingly palpable to those around us. Your spirit becomes a tangible presence, not merely metaphysical, but manifest in the physical realm. When you enter spaces, others sense a shift in the atmospheric tension, like the charged air before rainfall. The spiritual frequency you carry becomes increasingly resonant, affecting the quantum fabric of reality itself. Just as people in different faiths speak of their aura, your spirit influence takes on a tangible form. As your consciousness expands, your spirit's impact on your surroundings grows stronger.

Creation responds to the completeness it sees in you. A new creation life demands a new creation approach. Many people struggle and feel frustrated with their prayer life, but practicing ascension can help them unify it. It is about 'being' rather than 'doing'. Like a master conductor directing an orchestra, you establish laws and determine the currents of the spirit within those realms. The fabric of reality itself responds to your awakened state of consciousness. As with Moses, his ascension stirred the faith of the people, as they witnessed the tangible evidence of his ascension encounter.

When you awaken to your divine consciousness, it creates a ripple effect in the spiritual world around you. I've been fortunate enough to encounter spiritual figures like Moses, Ezekiel, and Abraham. Just as light bends around massive celestial bodies, reality itself seems to curve around those who have attained higher states of consciousness. Just like chatting with my brother, Justin Paul Abraham, who has personal experiences with Enoch. Justin speaks with powerful conviction, his authority rooted in his genuine spiritual substance. Ascension transcends a mere experience; it grows into a garment that envelops your essence, permanently altering your spiritual core and accompanying you on every journey.

DIVINE EMERGENCE

True power lies in embracing our divine essence,

Walking with purpose through existence.

As sons of God, we govern realms untold,

Each step awakening wisdom ancient and bold.

The old ways fade like shadows in the light,

As new creation dawns, brilliant, and bright.

For transformation calls us to ascend,

Where heaven's ways with earthly purpose blend.

Not by familiar paths shall we proceed.

But through divine alignment, shall we lead.

A new approach for this awakened state,

As we step forward to create.

In silence deep, our spirit's voice grows clear,

Revealing truths we're destined now to hear.

For in this sacred space of conscious grace,

We hold the power to transform this place.

YOUR INNER CELESTIAL LADDER

Exodus 19:10–11 NIV And the Lord said to Moses, "Go to the people and consecrate them today and tomorrow. Have them wash their clothes and be ready by the third day, because on that day the Lord will come down on Mount Sinai in the sight of all the people."

Moses went up, Yahweh came down. Yahweh positioned Moses as the Vav I, so that he could become the celestial staircase of the spirit realm.

From the **Zohar** "The Vav is the pillar extending from heaven to earth, uniting the realms above and below. It is the line that connects the higher and lower worlds, sustaining the flow of divine energy. When the Vav is complete, it brings together the male and female aspects, joining them as one. This union is the foundation of harmony in creation, for only when male and female are bound together does divine blessing flow freely, filling all worlds with light and sustaining life. Therefore, the Vav symbolises the channel through which the upper and lower realms are brought into alignment and unity."

You are the realm of release, like the keys mentioned in Matthew.

Matthew 18:18-20 NIV

"Truly I tell you, whatever you bind on earth will be bound in heaven, and whatever you loose on earth will be loosed in heaven. Again, truly I tell you that if two of you on earth agree about anything they ask for, it will be done for them by my Father in heaven."

Your decision and action activates heaven's resources, creating a momentum of provision, much like Jacob's revelation at Bethel where angels ascended and descended on the spiritual ladder (Genesis 28:12-13). This divine interaction pattern shows us how heaven's economy responds to earthly engagement.

Yahweh first positioned Moses in a state of ascension, then He came down and spoke to the people, the convergence of mortality with divinity. This demonstrates the divine protocol of elevation before revelation.

The spirit realm operates through you as its celestial highway, creating a living bridge between dimensions. As the passage in 1 Corinthians 6:19 states, "Do you not know that your bodies are temples of the Holy Spirit? "Your words carry tremendous weight because you have the authority to connect the entire spirit realm to yourself, reflecting the truth that we are His mirror image."

Tap into your inner celestial staircase and witness the convergence of the spirit realm with your destiny. Like Ezekiel's vision of the wheels within wheels (Ezekiel 1:15-21), there is a divine machinery of interconnected spiritual dimensions waiting to align with your purpose.

With each ascension, a ladder forms in your DNA strand, creating a spiritual pathway and increasing your awareness of position. This mirrors the pattern seen when Moses ascended and activated his DNA, the spiritual pathway formed within his consciousness of his mountain, which led to Yahweh's descent.

Engaging with ascension activates more pathways in your DNA, forming a beautiful tapestry of connectedness and oneness. This reflects Solomon's wisdom that 'The spirit of man is the lamp of the LORD, searching all his innermost parts' (Proverbs 20:27). Each activation creates new layers of spiritual perception, like the prophets of old who saw into multiple dimensions of reality.

These spiritual gateways in your being respond to intentional engagement, creating highways of Holiness

Isaiah 35:8 NIV 'And a highway will be there; it will be called the way of Holiness; it will be for those who walk on that way.'

As you ascend these internal mountains of encounters, like Moses, you mature into the living tabernacle where heaven's frequencies resonate with earth's matter, creating a symphony of divine expression through your being.

THE INNER CELESTIAL SPIRAL

Exodus 19:12–13 NIV 'Put limits for the people **around** the mountain and tell them, 'Be careful that you do not approach the mountain or touch the foot of it. Whoever touches the mountain is to be put to death. They are to be stoned or shot with arrows; not a hand is to be laid on them. No person or animal shall be permitted to live. Only when the ram's horn sounds a long blast may they approach the mountain.'

Ezekiel's vision of the temple reveals an architectural structure, a circular structure that ascends and expands, with chambers progressively increasing in both height and dimension, a divine spiral staircase reaching toward heaven (Ezekiel 41:7). This circular pattern is encoded in the Hebrew word מוּסָב" (mû·sāḇ)", the same term used in Yahweh's command to Moses about setting limits 'around 'the mountain. This is no mere coincidence, but a celestial blueprint unveiled.

A spiritual template of the temple encircled the base of Mount Sinai itself, a living architectural manifestation of divine order. The descendants, symbolised by the Hebrew letter 'ב' (bet), are called to step into this sacred blueprint. Like a seed contains the full pattern of the tree, this letter 'ב' represents the temple consciousness that must expand and grow. God's desire is to activate and cultivate their position as spiritual mountains.

As **Isaiah 2:2** declares, "In the last days, the mountain of the LORD's temple will be established as the highest of the mountains; it will be exalted above the hills, and all nations will stream to it."

To govern thrones on mountains and heavenly realms requires a willingness to expand the consciousness of one's own internal mountain - to become a living temple that grows in spiritual capacity and authority. Therefore, the Israelites couldn't approach the physical mountain without proper authorisation to engage with the temple blueprint. Their preparation was essential. The significance of this preparation is further illuminated in John 11:6, where Jesus, upon learning of Lazarus's illness, remained where he was for two days. This period of two days correlates with the Hebrew letter 'ב,' symbolising 'temple.' Jesus's seemingly delayed response wasn't negligence but divine alignment with temple protocol - waiting for perfect positioning of the temple structure that would serve as the vehicle for His manifest presence. This reflects Yahweh's instruction to Moses: consecrate the people for two days, approach mountain on the third day, the realm of redemption and resurrection.

The temple serves as the chosen vehicle through which Yahweh reveals His nature and government. It is both blueprint and living structure through which the realities of heavenly administration manifest. The prophetic cleansing through the cross enabled the Israelites to step fully into their role as temples of the Holy Spirit, as Paul later affirms in **1 Corinthians 6:19**: "Do you not know that your bodies are temples of the Holy Spirit, who is in you?"

The third day symbolises not just resurrection but complete transformation, the Israelites, now positioned within Christ and the finished work of the cross, could engage with Yahweh's plans at the mountain as resurrected ones, ascended light beings awakened to their true nature and purpose. While we exist simultaneously across multiple dimensions, our complete manifestation in the physical realm remains a progressive unveiling, a journey of expansion and growth into the fullness of our celestial identity.

This process of becoming mirrors the very structure of the temple itself - ever ascending, ever expanding, always anchored in the divine blueprint established at the mountain's base. It is a living paradox of simultaneous completion and continuous growth, much like the kingdom of God itself, already here, yet still unfolding in greater measure.

THE CELESTIAL
SOUND

Exodus 19:13 NIV 'Only when the **ram's horn** sounds a long blast may they approach the mountain.'

Why was the blowing of the shofar so profoundly significant? Its spiritual importance extends far beyond a ceremonial practice. The shofar serves as a frequency bridge between earthly and celestial realms, its reverberations creating waves to summon and invoke. When its trumpet pierces the veil between worlds, a cosmic announcement echoes that heaven invades the earth.

Psalm 47:5 "God has ascended amid shouts of joy, the LORD amid the sounding of trumpets."

As sons of God, we receive a divine mantle, but we must approach this celestial inheritance with holy wisdom and proper spiritual protocol. These protocols are not formalities but divine laws that establish living bridges of relationship and connection that we must honor with reverence. The sound of the shofar becomes a sonic embodiment of our covenant in Christ, its vibrations releasing the full spectrum of blessings that the blood of Christ has redeemed, opening ancient gates for Israel to enter their inheritance.

"Ascend, expand, and govern the thrones in heavenly realms by embracing the consciousness of your own mountain."

In the frequency of heaven, the shofar's sound announces with thunderous authority the covenant we have with Yahweh, preparing the hearts of the Israelites for divine engagement and making tangible their holy fear of the Lord. The cry of the shofar is a declaration of jubilee, framing seasons of freedom and deliverance. Each resonant blast activates angelic realms stationed at celestial gates, opening pathways for the sons of God to traverse dimensional portals.

"The voice of the shofar ascends and awakens another voice above, and they unite as one... When Israel below sounds the shofar, all the firmaments above are stirred and the voice rises to the supernal throne."

Here's a passage from the **Zohar** regarding the shofar sound "When the shofar is sounded below, all the voices called 'shofar' above are stirred. The voice ascends and is crowned above, awakening another voice, and they become interwoven with one another until they reach the place from which judgment issues. This stirring of voices brings about the balance of judgment and mercy, and each voice ascends, connecting below with above. The shofar blasts create harmony in the celestial realms, joining together all forces until they arrive at the place where divine judgment is shaped. Thus, the shofar blast below sets in motion the flow of mercy and compassion from above, affecting the judgments of the world."

The shofar's sound exists but as living, breathing entities of divine frequency. When these sound-entities are awakened through the shofar's blast, they rise like celestial pillars into the higher realms. As living sound waves between worlds, they possess an innate intelligence, recognising and responding to their mirror images in the superior dimensions. These heavenly sound-beings, eternally dwelling in the upper firmaments, descend to entangle the shofars sound, creating a divine dance of unification and activation. The merger of these sound-entities interweave, forming a living ladder of vibration, each entanglement creating a sound portal of ascent. Through this sacred acoustical marriage, the sound-entities become transformative agents, carrying prayers, intentions, and divine decrees between realms. They serve as the living embodiment of the Hebrew concept of מָשַׁךְ, literally drawing heaven and earth into alignment through their unified resonance.

"The voice of the shofar ascends and awakens another voice above, and they unite as one, creating a harmonious symphony. When Israel below sounds the shofar and ignites a cascade of movement in the heavens above, all the firmaments are stirred and the voice rises to the supernal throne."

The Hebrew texts speak of this sound as מָשַׁךְ (mā·šǎḵ) - "to draw up" - a linguistic key that unlocks understanding of its ascension properties. Through the masterful orchestration of trumpet sound, light, and frequency, Yahweh aligns cosmic forces to position the Israelites for their upward journey. Only when these sacred frequencies fill the air are they granted permission to approach the mountain and navigate its ascending pathways, each blast marking new territories of spiritual expansion and capability.

"Sound the shofar, ascend with reverence, and unlock the hidden mysteries in the treasuries of the morning."

When we understand that every frequency carries intention and every vibration opens specific spiritual doorways, we begin to grasp how sound becomes a living ladder between realms. The sacred name Yod Hey Vav Hey יהוה, when chanted with understanding, creates DNA-level resonance that activates dormant spiritual capacities.

The wisdom of sacred sound goes beyond what we hear with our ears. It resonates deep within our spirits. As it was for Moses on the mountain, so it remains for us: sound carries codes of ascension, frequencies of transformation. Each seeker must discover their unique resonance, the specific vibration that causes their spirit to rise and ascend their personal mountain of revelation. Within this revelation lies the gateway to uncharted spiritual realms and profound encounters with the divine.

The power of sacred sound surpasses mere auditory perception; it reverberates within the depths of our spirit. Sound holds the secrets of ascension and the catalyst for profound change. Every seeker must uncover their individual resonance, the precise vibration that elevates their spirit and propels them towards personal enlightenment.

THE MORNING OF OMENS

Exodus 19:16 NIV "On the **morning** of the third day there was thunder and lightning, with a thick cloud over the mountain, and a very loud trumpet blast. Everyone in the camp trembled."

Exodus 24:4, we read, "Moses then wrote down everything the Lord had said. He got up early the next **morning** and built an altar at the foot of the mountain and set up twelve stone pillars representing the twelve tribes of Israel."

'Morning' is the Hebrew word בֹּקֶר (bō·qĕr): and this is how the dictionary describes it to mean, **'sacrifice for omens, i.e., a sacrifice given to a deity in order to gain information normally kept secret.'**

I bet you didn't see that one coming?

Job 38: 12-13 AMP "Since your days began, have you ever commanded the morning, And caused the dawn to know its place, So that light may take hold of the corners of the earth And shake the wickedness out of it?"

The mystical art of commanding the morning בֹּקֶר reveals itself as a spiritual technology that allows us to entangle the future we create. This calls upon the sons of God to participate in the daily renewal of creation. In Jewish mysticism, particularly in Kabbalistic thought, the morning symbolises the daily recreation of the world. It is when divine light breaks through the darkness of chaos, similar to the primordial phrase "Let there be light."

The Hebrew word בֹּקֶר holds the secret of divination and prophecy. However, it is not about fortune-telling. Instead, it is an ascension that draws a curtain between the visible and invisible realms, allowing us to step into the beginning. When we "command the morning," we engage in a cosmic partnership. We stand between night and day, chaos and order, concealment and revelation. This practice requires us to align our consciousness with God's creative force that renews all existence. By doing so, we can shape reality through our aligned will and divine permission. The mystical entanglement of commanding the morning is a daily ascension that allows us to participate in the ongoing emergence of creation, transforming dawn into a portal for divine co-creation.

"When the world was created, a supernal, concealed light

shone forth. This light is hidden away, yet it emerges each day to renew creation, illuminating the worlds above and below..."

The Zohar describes that each day, the world is renewed by the primordial light, the first light that emanated at creation. This light is hidden but continuously flows to sustain all existence. Were it not for this renewal by the hidden light, the world could not endure for even a single moment. Each morning, this divine light renews creation, maintaining the balance of all realms and filling the world with the energy necessary to sustain life. Thus, the light of the first morning is concealed, yet it shines anew each day, ensuring the survival and harmony of all creation.

The morning realm is a place of divine convergence, positioning you to embrace hidden truths and bask in divine bliss. The clamour of the earthly realm subsides, while the resounding chorus of the spirit realm rises, enveloping you in a symphony of celestial vibrations.

When you fully embrace your role as an Elohim during the process of ascension, you tap into the profound knowledge of Yahweh and gain a deep understanding of the realm of בֹּקֶר (bō·qěr.)

Ascension is not about striving to accomplish something, but rather about uncovering hidden mysteries. It is about embracing your true essence and identity. While servants focus on doing, sons simply exist and settle into their authentic selves. When you open yourself up to this state of being, you emit a powerful frequency that attracts creation towards you, recognising the divine blueprint within. The sons, who carry the blueprints, are the ones who practice ascension because they embody this state of being.

THE PRIMORDIAL GATE

Exodus 19:17 NIV "Then Moses led the people out of the camp to meet with God, and they stood at the **foot** of the mountain."

The Hebrew word for 'foot 'is תַּחְתִּי (tăh·tî) and means '**lower, below, underneath, i.e., pertaining to a space below another point of reference like depths, the below**

region.'

Sefer Yetzirah 1:5 Aryeh Kaplan's Translation: "He set them in Tohu (formless) and Bohu (empty), placed them in the emptiness and the void. He set them in the depths, placed them in the chaos, and formed them as the pillars of existence."

At Mount Sinai's foot, the Israelites stood on the edge of primordial creation. This place, known as תַּחְתִּי (Tachti), marked the boundary between the ordered world and the enigmatic Tahom—the deep ancient waters of Genesis. Positioned at the gateway between form and formlessness, they embodied a mystical state, existing "below" or "underneath," which aligns with the teachings of the Sefer Yetzirah about Yahweh placing foundational letters in the chaotic Tohu and Bohu that preceded creation. This signifies their presence in the primordial chaos, where unshaped potential lies. In a parallel to their physical location at the mountain's base, they stood at the precipice of formlessness, gazing into Tahom, ready to receive the sacred structure of ascension that would transform chaos into cosmic order. The double Tav (ת) that embraces the word תַּחְתִּי creates a sacred vessel, its dual presence speaking to the completion of both physical exodus and spiritual preparation. In Hebrew mysticism, Tav represents covenant and the seal of creation, and its double appearance here suggests a sealed chamber where transformation becomes possible. Like the two cherubim guarding Eden's gates, these twin Tavs stand as arcing gates at the threshold of revelation.

The mountain itself takes on a new significance, becoming a living axis, a cosmic pillar that connects the depths of Tahom to the heights of the divine throne. Each step upward represents a journey through the celestial hierarchies, traversing the realms of angels, thrones, and principalities in the kingdom of God. Just as the Sefer Yetzirah speaks of God forming letters into "pillars of existence," the revelation at Sinai established the pillars of cosmic order through the giving of the Torah. In this moment, the people stood at the intersection of multiple dimensions of reality—their consciousness grounded in the chaos of Tahom while their spirits reached towards the divine throne above. This positioning created the perfect condition for divine transitioning, as they existed between the realms of formed and unformed order and chaos, human and divine.

Standing at the mountain's base, human consciousness, born from the primordial waters of creation, faces a threshold of transformation. This journey, an ascent through the celestial spheres, symbolises the movement from the microcosm to the macrocosm, leading to ultimate revelation and mystery.

The word תַּחְתִּי thus becomes not merely a geographical marker but a mystical blueprint for divine-human encounter. The "emptiness and void" mentioned in Sefer Yetzirah becomes, at Sinai, filled with divine presence. The mountain's foot becomes the sacred chamber where transformation occurs – where the physical realm is elevated to spiritual significance through divine indwelling. This demonstrates how the seemingly lowest point (תַּחְתִּי) can become the highest point of divine-human connection, embodying the paradox that the deepest depths contain the potential for the greatest heights of spiritual elevation.

A SUMMARY OF THE JOURNEY SO FAR: FROM DESERT TO DIVINE COUNCIL

Through Moses' extraordinary journey at Mount Sinai, we discover truths about our own potential for divine encounters and spiritual elevation.

The Hebrew language reveals three distinct stages of ascension, each opening new dimensions of spiritual experience. We begin with לה (Lah), where divine breath awakens our dormant spiritual identity. Like Moses at the burning bush, this initial awakening comes through intimate encounters with God's presence. This breath becomes our vehicle of ascension, drawing us higher while releasing what no longer serves our elevation.

As we mature, we encounter נשא (Nasa), where we discover the eternal echoes within our spiritual DNA. This stage reveals our inherent drive toward transcendence, awakening abilities encoded within us since creation. Finally, we reach סלק (Salak), where we step into realms of heavenly governance and dimensional authority. Here, we don't merely visit higher dimensions; we inhabit and administer them as sons of God.

As you contemplate these stages of ascension, you discover they serve as keys, unlocking both consciousness and authority. Like the trumpet blast at Sinai, these experiences catalyse your spirit, propelling you into higher and deeper realms while transforming your very DNA. Within this journey, you step into a profound inheritance as the Mazzaroth, carrying blessings spoken over each tribe through bloodline inheritance in Christ.

The desert where Moses encountered God wasn't merely a barren landscape but represented the "mouth" of divine frequency, a place where heaven's voice unfolds on earth. Similarly, we each carry this potential for divine encounter within us. We embody the mountain, becoming the very structure of ascension itself. We navigate through heavenly realms where gods and thrones dwell, realms eagerly awaiting the activation of our ascension ladder and the release of mandates for our process.

Central to this journey is understanding spiritual garments, not physical clothing, but vibrational interfaces that allow us to harmonise with different dimensional frequencies. These garments enable us to navigate spiritual realms while carrying specific authority markers. They represent graduated levels of consciousness and spiritual capacity that we mature into as we ascend.

The "matrix of ascension" emerges as a cosmic womb where infinite potential crystallises into reality. This sacred space serves as both incubator and catalyst, where divine possibilities gestate before manifesting in our world. Within this matrix, we undergo profound transformation, downloading revelation and calibrating our consciousness to higher frequencies.

During ascension, we encounter angels of fire who assist in transformation, measurement, and expansion, just as they drew Moses to the burning bush at Sinai. In the spiritual sense, every ascension intertwines with this divine fire, creating opportunities for transformation and governance. These encounters aren't just about reaching higher realms; they're about receiving sceptres of authority to govern in the spirit realm.

The burning bush encounter reveals another crucial dimension, access to divine councils where celestial beings gather in heavenly governance. These councils remain active realms where we're invited to participate in spiritual administration. Through Christ, we have the authority to engage with these realms and receive heavenly mandates.

Sound plays a vital role in this journey, particularly through the shofar's blast. These sacred frequencies create living bridges between dimensions, carrying divine intention and opening spiritual portals. The sounds themselves become living entities, intelligent carriers of heavenly frequency that facilitate movement between realms.

Then, we learn about "commanding the morning", a daily opportunity to participate in divine creativity and renewal. Each dawn presents a portal for co-creation with God, where we can shape reality through aligned will and divine permission.

As we mature in ascension, we unlock more doors that lead to tangible manifestations in our physical surroundings. From the fire of our mountain, Jesus speaks to us face-to-face, inviting us to position ourselves within that divine fire and explore the various fires in heavenly realms as we continue to progress.

In this journey of ascension, we are invited to engage with spiritual entanglements, celestial beings, and divine councils. We are urged to seek Yahweh's guidance regarding the specific realms He wants us to govern, be it in our work, family, or in deepening our relationship with Jesus. This process involves discovering which angelic beings we should engage with and comprehending the responsibilities associated with our assigned realms.

By Christ's finished work, all of God's sons now have access to these realms of experience and authority. Instead of simply admiring Moses' experiences from a distance, we are called to even greater encounters. Through training our spiritual senses, we can perceive and interact with multiple dimensions of reality, bringing heaven's perspective into every sphere of influence.

Through this expanded journey, we recognise that ascension isn't just about personal elevation - it's about creation itself looking to us for fulfilment. As we step into these realms of authority and presence, each experience becomes a stepping stone toward greater manifestation of heaven's reality on earth.

"The process of ascension unlocks the divine power within, transforming DNA and propelling us to higher realms. Embracing our role as sons of God, we become the mountain of ascension, navigating heavenly realms of remembrance"

THE MOUNTAIN OF ASCENSION

In Sinai's flame, the spirit takes flight, a burning bush, a sacred light.

לה (Lah) awakens, breath divine, the spark of God in hearts enshrined. Released from chains, we rise, we soar, through realms unbound, we hunger for more.

נשא (Nasa) hums, an ancient song, transcendence calls where we belong. Eternal echoes stir the fire, awakening our deep desire. Within us flows the endless stream, the essence of creation's dream.

סלק (Salak) crowns the sovereign call, where sons of God inhabit all. Not seekers now, but rulers stand with sceptres forged by heaven's hand. The mountain burns, the veil is torn, in divine fire, the soul is born.

The desert speaks with heaven's sound, where realms unseen in light are found. Garments of frequency we wear, vibrations calling us to dare. Through morning's song, we shape the day, as creation bends to heaven's sway.

Ascend, O son, the time is near, To wield the flame, to silence fear. For all creation groans to see, The sons of God in majesty.

ASCENSION ACTIVATION

Imagine yourself standing at the base of a majestic mountain, a representation of your personal Mount Zion. Let your consciousness sink deep into the mystical realm of tahom תְּהוֹם, where the three stages of ascension await your discovery. Sense the divine breath of לה (Lah) stirring within you, awakening your dormant spiritual identity just as it first awakened in Moses at the burning bush.

As you gaze upon the mountain, witness the seraphim, the angels of fire, surrounding you. These are the same angels of fire who drew Moses to his divine encounter, now present to assist in your transformation. Focus your visualisation on the Vav ו symbol, positioned at the centre of the mountain, symbolising your DNA in a state of ascension. Feel the stage of נשא (Nasa) activating within you, awakening the eternal echoes encoded in your spiritual DNA since creation.

Gradually move closer to the mountain, and as you stand at its base, remember that you are the ב, the structure of the temple. Look down and visualise yourself standing within the realm of tahom. Surrounding you are thrones occupied by the divine council, the Elohim themselves, closely watching as you step into your inheritance, embodying the Mazzaroth. Feel your spirit expanding and growing, becoming one with the mountain itself. You embody the Vav ו symbol, and the angels of fire ascend your DNA ladder, moving upwards through your spiritual garments - those vibrational interfaces that allow you to harmonise with different dimensional frequencies.

From the depths of tahom, sense the mysteries of the kingdom ascending your DNA staircase. Your consciousness expands into סלק (Salak), where you step into realms of heavenly governance. Witness a gateway opening within the mountain and behold Moses approaching you. He wraps his mantle of ascension around you, not just a physical covering, but a spiritual garment carrying specific authority markers. Remember that you possess your own unique blueprint, like Moses' mantle, that represents the pattern of a divine encounter.

As you engage in that experience, allow your spirit to be activated within the matrix of ascension - this cosmic womb where infinite potential crystallises into reality. Enveloped in the mantle, listen to the resonating sound of a shofar. These sacred frequencies create living bridges between dimensions. Tune in to these unique frequencies and find the one that resonates with your spirit's calling to govern in the spirit realm.

Now, imagine another shofar sound, originating from the summit of the mountain. It signifies the unveiling of Yahweh's manifest presence and your invitation to the divine council. Immerse yourself in the realm, envisioning your spirit piercing through the dense mist of His divine presence. Embrace the gentle caress of water streaming down your face, each droplet a vivid recollection of His essence intertwining with your being, awakening your position within the heavenly governance.

The resplendence of Yahweh dances and swirls both around and within you. Hear the reverberating rumble of thunder, and witness the breathtaking brilliance of lightning, the frequencies resonating from His omnipotent presence. Notice in awe as the essence of א bursts forth from His divine being, commanding the morning and participating in divine creativity. Gaze into the beyond, perceiving the vibrant spiritual activity that surrounds you in these celestial councils.

Traverse effortlessly between realms, encountering Yahweh face to face in this divine council setting. Seraphim gracefully encircle both you and Him, whilst majestic thrones align themselves around, beholding the magnificent encounter that sets your spirit, soul, and body ablaze. The mysteries continue to flow through your spirit, erupting like a volcano, downloading revelation and calibrating your consciousness to higher frequencies.

The dense cloud of glory envelops you as you engage in this face-to-face encounter with Yahweh within His council. In that sacred space, open your eyes and expand your consciousness into this new realm of authority. Feel the weight of your spiritual sceptre as you step into your role in spiritual administration. We want to dwell in that realm and operate from there continuously, bringing heaven's perspective into every sphere of influence.

May this activation ignite revelation within you, transforming your DNA and awakening you to your profound inheritance in Christ.

THE MYSTERY OF IMAGINATION

Colossians 3:1-2 NIV 'Since, then, you have been raised with Christ, set your hearts on things above, where Christ is, seated at the right hand of God. Set your minds on things above, not on earthly things.'

The Mirror Bible describes the above verse like this - 'See yourselves co-raised with Christ! Now ponder with persuasion the consequence of your co-inclusion in Him. Relocate yourselves mentally! Engage your thoughts with throne room realities where you are co-seated with Christ in the executive authority of God's right hand. Become affectionately acquainted with throne room thoughts will keep you from being distracted again by the earthly.'

Use your imagination as a key to relocation. Cultivate your imagination, for it is not a gate for pretending, but a powerful means of manifesting reality. Your imagination transcends mere pretence but transforms into a formidable force capable of shaping reality itself. Through it, you can gain a deeper understanding of the spiritual realm and envision the most extraordinary dreams imaginable.

Ephesians 2:6 Mirror Bible

'We are co-included in his resurrection. We are also elevated in his ascension to be equally present in the throne room of the heavenly realm where we are co-seated with him in his executive authority. We are fully represented in Christ Jesus.'

Activate your imagination from your seat in Christ, the heavenly realms. Your imagination ascension is the process of unlocking the divine reality of the throne room in your immediate surroundings. It surpasses the perceived reality of the world around you. Expand your imagination with thoughts of the throne room and avoid being distracted by earthly realities. The scripture aims to rapture you into the complete mindset, will, and emotions of Yahweh through the ascension process.

When a person cleaves in imagination to the Master of the Universe, they engage in an act of spiritual alignment, harmonising the divine encounters. These encounters representing the various attributes and manifestations of Yahweh, converge and interconnect, forming a unified and balanced structure within you. This inner alignment mirrors the unity of the divine realms and sets the stage for a transformative spiritual ascent.

Through this harmonisation, your mind and spirit are lifted beyond the bounds of the material world. Your thoughts transcend the ordinary, journeying to the supernal throne—a realm of sublime and infinite light. Here, you perceive the splendour of the mountain, a mystical vision described as embodying the unification of all realms and dimensions. Your mountain is not a static image but a living, dynamic process, filled with radiant light and the interplay of the divine attributes. It reveals the intricate connection between all levels of existence, illustrating how each part contributes to the wholeness of creation.

As you ascend, thought and imagination become vital for this adventure. They serve as a ladder, enabling you to climb higher and higher into the realms of divine insight. Imagination, often dismissed as a faculty of fantasy, here transforms into a mystical realm, capable of beholding the brilliance of the divine mountain.

Your imagination not only witnesses this cosmic interplay but becomes a participant in it. Your thoughts and intentions align with Yahweh's divine will and act as a conduit for the flow from heavenly realms. In this state, you unite heaven and earth. Your imagination embodies the unification, becoming a vessel through which divine imagery flows.

Imagination is an invitation to live a life of alignment, awareness, and purpose, drawing from the infinite wellspring of mystical vision.

The **Zohar** describes imagination this way... "When a person cleaves to the Holy One in thought and intention, they draw down the light of the upper worlds, merging the heavenly with the earthly. Through this, they become a channel for divine blessings to flow into the world."

THE MYSTERY OF IMAGINATION

THE SACRED POWER OF IMAGINATION: THOUGHTS THAT SHAPE REALITY

Proverbs 23:7 "As a man thinks in his heart, so is he", speaks to a profound truth about human consciousness and our ability to shape reality through thought. This sacred principle finds expression in the three distinct but interweaving paths of imagination that shape our journey through life.

The Three Paths of Divine Imagination:

1. The Co-Creators Vision (Projective Imagination)

In the same way that God created the world by saying "Let there be light," we also possess the ability to imagine and bring things into existence. It is through this process that we can envision and manifest our desired future, whether it be constructing a bridge or earning a degree. Transforming the unseen into reality resembles a builder's imagination, visualising the final product from the start.

2. The Creator's Dance (Creative Imagination)

The second path reflects the continuous act of creation, in which Yahweh collaborates with humanity to shape and transform reality. Similar to a sculptor who starts with a block of clay and uncovers the inherent form, or a writer who witnesses their characters come alive, this imaginative process intertwines vision and emergence. It serves as a reminder of how God infused life into Adam, starting with a vision while embracing the enigma of free will and personal growth.

3. The Oracle's Gift (Receptive Imagination)

The path of mystery that lies before us is undeniably captivating. It is defined by those moments of sudden enlightenment, where a flash of insight brings forth new possibilities. Like Joseph's vivid dreams or the prophetic visions that Ezekiel experienced. These divine inspirations are not the result of our careful planning, but our willingness to be open and let Jesus guide our dreams. Imagination, you see, is unlimited. It serves as a channel to higher realms of vision.

The paths we speak of may seem separate, but in reality, they come together like streams into a river. Practical planners may find unexpected inspiration, while intuitive artists must engage in methodical creation. This reflects how God plans and allows for emergence, speaks clearly and moves mysteriously.

The power of imagination goes beyond daydreaming; it involves actively taking part in the process of creation. When we envision our future selves, we are taking part in a profound act of co-creation. As the Proverb implies, our thoughts not only influence our actions, but also shape our very being.

Dreams serve as a minute yet profound gateway to prophetic insight, representing a small but significant fraction of true prophecy's essence. They function as celestial portals, through which sacred understanding descends into the human consciousness. Those who are in Christ have the spiritual elevation to be vessels attuned to higher dimensions.

Furthermore, cosmic understanding reveals itself not through physical striving, but rather descends spontaneously from transcendent spheres. Like sudden illumination piercing darkness, this wisdom penetrates directly into your innermost being, bypassing ordinary consciousness to touch the deepest aspects of human awareness.

Yahweh gave us the gift of imagination, not for indulging in fantasies, but as a mystical key for personal transformation and unfolding. It is through our thoughts that we shape our reality. This truth, with its weighty responsibility and divine blessing, empowers us to participate in our own evolution of becoming through the mystical practice of imagination. In this manner, imagination takes on a spiritual significance, serving as a pathway to join in the continuous act of creation, guided by both divine inspiration and deliberate intention.

DIVINE
MANIFESTATIONS

Exodus 19:18 NIV "Mount Sinai was covered with **smoke**, *because* the Lord descended on it in fire. The **smoke** billowed up from it like smoke from a furnace, and the whole mountain trembled violently."

This event is described in Hebrew by emphasising that the mountain completely vanished from sight. The enveloping smoke symbolised Yahweh's unfolding presence, evoking reverence and showcasing the emotion and weightiness of the nature of God. The smoke was a profound manifestation of the glory of God's presence transitioning from the spiritual collapsing into the physical realm. An extraordinary phenomenon!

In Hebrew, the term used for "because" is "פָּנֶה (pā·nĕ(h))," which translates to **"face."** The mention of the Lord's descent refers to Yahweh's face unfolding itself on the mountain. Imagine that picture! As the Israelites watched the smoke, they witnessed the multidimensional manifestation of God's face, accompanied by unfathomable sounds and frequencies. In His appearance and presence, God unveiled many dimensions of His being. When Moses encountered the smoke, it represented the hidden realms of Yahweh's intimacy surrounding him. Their interaction was a blending, where the distinction between Yahweh's face and Moses' face disappeared. This face-to-face meeting marked Moses' ascension matrix. In the same way, as we unlock ascension realms and reach the spiritual heights, not through works but a becoming within ourselves, God's desires become ours. We become one with His perception and senses. The utmost importance lies in our reverence for God and our humility, as everything revolves around Him. He longs for every aspect of our lives to hold meaning and significance, seeking a deep connection that erases any sense of separation. This journey of being enveloped in Yahweh opens our minds, showing us that there is no separation between us and Him. We are united in Christ, entangled in the oneness of His image. Through the ascension matrix, we understand Jesus is the unity of the divine and yourself, both embodying the same eternal consciousness living in you.

In **Numbers 12:6-8**. "And he said, listen to my words. When there is a prophet among you, I, the Lord, **reveal** myself to them in visions. I speak to them in dreams. But this is not true of my servant Moses. He is **faithful** in all my house. With him I speak face 'into' face and not in riddles. He sees the form of the Lord."

In this scripture, the Hebrew word for **"to"** translates to **"into."** The prophets receive knowledge of Yahweh, but Moses, through his face-to-face encounter, received both revelation and mystery. This distinction between knowledge and revelation is of great significance. Moses proved his faithfulness in all aspects of God's house. The Hebrew word אָמוֹן ('ā·môn) interprets 'faithful' as a craftsman. Why a craftsman?

"Moses was faithful as a steward of the kingdom's mysteries and therefore God entrusted him with the secrets of the mountain."

In the great mystical traditions of the world, the image of the mountain often symbolises the sacred journey of ascent - both an external path and an inner awakening. This journey is a transformative process of becoming. The summit is a state of consciousness, a realm where mystery and revelation meet. At the heart of this journey lies a secret key, that, those who ascend the mountain, become keepers of the mysteries, entrusted with the task of stewarding divine wisdom advancing all of creation.

A DIRECT
DOWNLOAD

The mystical writings describe Moses as a figure of unparalleled spiritual stature. While prophets received visions and dreams, often cloaked in riddles and symbols, Moses stood in direct communion with Yahweh. He was described as gazing "into the mirror that shines," beholding the Infinite without distortion. This extraordinary privilege was not merely granted to Moses, he matured into it. He was described as "faithful in all the house of God," not only in his actions but in his stewardship of the mysteries entrusted to him.

Moses was a spiritual craftsman, shaping the divine mysteries into tangible forms: the laws, the Tabernacle, and the rituals that would guide Israel. To be a keeper of the mysteries is to engage with the creativity of Yahweh, unfolding potential into substance. Each step upward is both a movement into the unknown and an act of trust, trust that Jesus has placed within us the capacity to receive and steward great mysteries.

The **Zohar** compares the righteous as "builders of the divine palace," whose spiritual entanglements shape and influence the cosmos. Every act of righteousness, every moment of contemplation, becomes a stone in the supernal structure, contributing to a harmonious reality. The goal isn't just individual enlightenment, but healing and elevating the entire creation. It is a sacred partnership, a co-creative dance with Yahweh.

As we continue our ascent, we become aware that the path before us is not a straightforward one, but a spiral that takes us further into our own being while bringing us closer to the Infinite. This journey calls for surrender, a willingness to let go of our preconceived notions and limited viewpoints, and instead embrace the unfolding mysteries. Like Moses, we become craftsman, moulding the revelations we receive into something that others can share and comprehend. It is through giving that we receive, and through revelation, that the doors to our inner sanctum are opened.

It is here where mystery lives, hidden even from the most learned until they are ready to receive it. Mystery is not simply knowledge we have not yet attained; it is a reality that transcends understanding, inviting us into communion rather than mastery. Moses, standing at the threshold of the Infinite, received not only knowledge but also the mystery of God's essence. This is the privilege of the faithful craftsman: to hold both revelation and mystery, shaping them into forms that illuminate without diminishing their depth.

To ascend your mountain is to embrace the sacred responsibility of stewardship. Unlocking deeper realms of consciousness, you become a vessel for divine wisdom. This is not a passive role, but an active, creative one. You are called to shape what you receive into something that can bless and uplift the world. This path requires courage and humility. The deeper you ascend, the more you realise how much remains veiled.

Through this adventurous journey of ascent, Jesus transforms you into a faithful craftsman, a co-creator with Him. You become a builder of the palace, a guardian of the mysteries, and a channel through which the hidden light flows into the world. More than just a place of enlightenment, your mountain becomes a powerful symbol of the unity of creation, a unity that you are now charged with governing and leading.

MATURING INTO THE DOWNLOADS

As an Elohim, you gain exposure to the divine realms and Yahweh cultivates your maturity for governance and rulership, unveiling more mysteries and expanding your capacity for stewardship with each step of your ascension. As we ascend, we unlock access to the celestial realms of תהום (Tehom) the deep. Within this realm, the divine mandates are given to us and we are entrusted with responsibilities that harmonise with our celestial calling.

Because Moses was faithful in all of Yahweh's house, Yahweh granted him access to these celestial realms. He stewarded the mysteries with the maturity of one who has become one with the Kingdom. This is the essence of true maturity—when something becomes an integral part of your being, you embody its very nature. The revelation of your identity is aligning with what heaven already knows about you. Maturity echoes oneness.

In this state, Moses became a living embodiment of the divine mysteries he stewarded. The revelation of his identity was not a mere intellectual understanding, but a deep alignment with what heaven already knew about him. It was a merging of his earthly existence with the eternal truths of the celestial realms.

Exodus 19:18 NIV '...The smoke billowed up from it like smoke from a furnace, and the whole mountain trembled violently.'

This divine manifestation reveals two dimensions of the glory fire encountered during ascension:

1. The Purifying Fire: This sacred flame explores the depths of your being, compassionately seeking impurities. Its purpose is to refine, not judge, as it aims to strengthen your connection with the lover of your soul. As you delve deeper, God thoroughly examines your heart. Embrace this process with joy, for it is not about finding faults, but about guiding you into divine realms. While we may have encountered a similar realm in the measuring phase, furthering the journey will bring to light forgotten issues that we have learned to live with and accepted as part of our daily lives. This purifying fire, while sometimes uncomfortable, is God's way of removing obstacles that prevent deeper spiritual connection and encounters.

2. The Transforming Fire: Following purification, this fire reshapes your essence, aligning you with your divine purpose and the next level of spiritual evolution. As the purifying fire completes its work, the radiant transforming fire emerges, its intense heat reshaping you into your divine calling and propelling you to the next level of being.

Deuteronomy 4:36 'Out of heaven He let you hear His voice, that He might instruct you; on earth He showed you His great fire, and you heard His words out of the midst of the fire.'

Often, this fire serves to help us embrace divine instruction and commands. Without transformation, we risk misinterpreting and misapplying these divine directives, potentially causing harm. The fires of purification and transformation are part of a maturity process, growing our capacity for faithful stewardship of the kingdom, just as with Moses. It's an exciting process of shaping our primordial existence in heaven, manifest on earth.

THE SYMPHONY OF ASCENSION

Exodus 19:19, 'As the sound of the trumpet **grew louder and louder**, Moses spoke and the voice of **God** answered him.'

In Hebrew, 'grew louder, הָלַךְ ' (hā·lăk) - means to **'transition'**. The sound of the shofar pierced the firmaments, its resonance dancing through creation. With each frequency, it awakened the upper worlds, summoning the celestial realms to unite with you.

It was sound infused with the vibration of divine intent, a cosmic signal opening gates long sealed. It was as if the breath of the Infinite flowed through the shofar, unlocking mysteries hidden since the foundation of creation.

The shofar's sound served as a cosmic key to transition Moses into higher spiritual dimensions. This auditory ascension teaches the ascension journey is not merely visual, but deeply auditory, sound, and frequency. The sounds of celestial realms empower the spirit to reach ecstatic states of being and knowing.

Don't focus only on visuals. The auditory experience - the sound being released as you ascend - is equally vital. This sound facilitates your transition into realms where you can release from your spiritual gate. It's this transition that enabled Moses to speak, accessing words connected to higher realms.

We're entering an age of intense spiritual experiences reminiscent of John's invitation in the Book of Revelation to "come up here." Therefore, teaching ascension is so crucial - God wants to reveal knowledge hidden from the world. He desires to show you formulas, algorithms and mysteries. These aren't just abstract spiritual concepts, but have practical applications in your workplace, relationships, and daily life. They provide a spiritual advantage in navigating earthly existence.

As the sound ascends, the notes entangle your DNA into a deeper spiral. Each tone is a step, lifting you beyond the limitations of the physical. When the voice rises and harmonises, it aligns with frequencies of the supernal realms. Each note corresponds to a gate of wisdom, a portal through which the sons may entangle the mysteries of the cosmos.

Ascending through sound is being immersed in the very pulse of creation. It is to hear not with the ears but with the spirit, attuned to the voice of Elohim. Yahweh desires to share the secrets of His word and the mysteries of existence with those prepared to listen, attuned to their inner sanctuary, to the sacred frequency, the song of creation.

THE MYSTERY DNA OF ELOHIM AND YAHWEH

Exodus 19:19, "As the sound of the trumpet grew louder and louder, Moses spoke and the **voice** of **God** answered him."

It's essential to understand that this wasn't Yahweh speaking, but Elohim, embodying God in His full, unified being. The term 'voice' (לוק, qol) is often associated with thunder, the primordial sound resonating through creation. Moses heard a voice echoing with the power of thunder, creating a symphony of divine frequencies. This wasn't just sound; it was the divine imprint of creation itself. The God who spoke to Moses was Elohim, the God of infinite potential and multifaceted unity. However, when God summoned Moses, it was the Lord—Yahweh—meaning covenant, relationship, and intimacy.

This distinction is vital in understanding the interplay between Elohim and Yahweh. When Elohim (God in plurality) speaks, it's the harmonic convergence of divine voices. Elohim speaks as the Creator, the cosmic architect who weaves the threads of existence. This is the God who said, "Let Us make man in Our image, after Our likeness" (**Genesis 1:26**), revealing the plurality within unity. Elohim is the divine DNA, the collective sound of I Am Who I Am (אֶהְיֶה אֲשֶׁר אֶהְיֶה, Ehyeh Asher Ehyeh). When Moses was summoned, however, it was Yahweh, the Tetragrammaton, the name signifying the God of covenant intimacy, who called him. Yahweh represents the sacred whisper of love and closeness bridging the infinite to the finite, the eternal to the temporal.

When Yahweh speaks, it's the intimate whisper of the Beloved going face into face with you. Discern between these voices, for each carries a unique mandate and mystery. When God (Elohim) speaks, there's more than one voice at play. When Yahweh speaks, its focus is covenant intimacy.

Mystical writings illuminate this dynamic by stating that the names of God are not merely linguistic markers, but energy codes. Elohim represents the attribute of Gevurah (strength, boundaries), while Yahweh encompasses Tiferet (beauty, harmony). Together, they harmonise the tension between the transcendent and the immanent. Elohim is the secret of creation, the architect of the worlds, while Yahweh is the light entering into creation, illuminating and giving it life. This interplay reveals Elohim as the DNA of the divine, structured, powerful, encompassing multiplicity—while Yahweh is the breath of life animating and drawing us into intimate communion. The cross, through Jesus, is the one that unifies and activates primordial memory and existence.

When Elohim (God in plurality) speaks, it's the harmonic convergence of divine voices. Each vibration is a thread in the cosmic tapestry, resonating with the frequencies of creation. The Sefer Yetzirah, the Book of Formation, describes how the universe is constructed through the Hebrew letters, each carrying the vibrational essence of Elohim's voice. "He engraved with them... the foundation of all things". These letters are not merely symbols but the spiritual DNA of existence, encoded with the divine frequencies that Moses heard at Sinai.

When Yahweh speaks, however, it is an intimate whisper, the still small voice (1 Kings 19:12) that beckons us into face-to-face encounters. Yahweh is the name that reveals the divine longing for a relationship, the voice that spoke to Moses from the burning bush, calling him by name (Exodus 3:4). Note at the burning bush Elohim called to Moses, but on the mountain it was Yahweh that summoned Moses, emphasising that Elohim and Yahweh carry different gates and pathways, yet one. Yahweh is the aspect of God that seeks to draw humanity closer, to bridge the infinite chasm and unite us with the divine presence. This is the voice of the covenant, the tender call to "know and be known." Jesus is the manifestation of that covenant.

To discern between these voices is to engage with the mysteries of divine revelation. When Elohim speaks, it invites us to explore the vastness of creation, the infinite realms and dimensions of the spirit. It is the voice of the Creator, the one who reveals the hidden pathways of the cosmos. But when Yahweh speaks, it is an invitation into the 'panim el panim', face-to-face intimacy that Moses experienced when "the Lord spoke to Moses face to face, as one speaks to a friend" (**Exodus 33:11**).

The path of ascension is not a rigid formula, but a labyrinthine journey into the divine heart. The Tree of Life itself is composed of interconnected pathways, each representing a unique aspect of divine wisdom and experience. Jesus reveals this as the ultimate Tree of Life. Elohim speaks through these pathways, revealing the structure of creation and the laws that govern it. Yahweh, however, is the essence that animates the journey, the intimate companion who walks with us through the labyrinth.

The revelations drawn from Moses' profound encounters hold the keys to unlocking our own ascension matrix. The DNA of Elohim reveals the infinite potential within us, encoded in the image of the divine. The call of Yahweh invites us into covenant intimacy, to discover the depths of divine love and to ascend through relationship. Jesus, the embodiment of all, resonates this through redemption and completion.

Keep in mind that the path to ascension has no set formula, it's a captivating labyrinth with infinite possibilities. The revelations drawn from Moses' profound encounters hold the keys to unlocking your own ascension matrix, but each expedition is a mesmerising tapestry of individuality.

THE DARKNESS
AND THE INNER
MYSTERY

Exodus 20:21 "The people remained at a distance, while Moses approached the **thick darkness** where God was."

When Moses approached the thick darkness, the dwelling of Elohim, he entered not just a physical phenomenon, but a dimensional gateway. This mirrors the biblical account where the people stood at a distance while Moses entered this mysterious realm. It speaks to the eternal pattern of divine encounter where Moses wrapped himself in a robe of darkness, entangling a sacred chamber of supernal wisdom. Unfortunately, this moment highlights a tragic missed opportunity for the Israelites. Yahweh had positioned them all to ascend and engage His presence, but they focused on the wrong aspects, misinterpreting the situation. They defaulted to sending Moses as an intermediary, a pattern unfortunately mirrored in much of modern church culture.

Every believer is a new creation, a son of God, a king, priest, and prophet in the order of Melchizedek. As a result, they possess the same capability as anyone in ministry to receive divine revelation. This viewpoint challenges the tendency to place religious leaders on pedestals. While we acknowledge the importance of leadership in ministry, our approach to spiritual guidance differs. The underlying message is clear: there is no significant distinction between the spiritual leader's ascent and that of any sincere seeker. The only variables that differ are belief and the willingness to fully embrace their sonship.

Deuteronomy 4:11 says, "You came near and stood at the foot of the mountain while it blazed with fire to the very heavens, with black clouds and deep darkness."

We see a progression in Moses' experiences. Initially, he encountered a cloud, but later, he approached the thick darkness of Elohim. This thick darkness, described as black clouds in Deuteronomy, embodies the intensity of spiritual activity. Moses' journey presents a remarkable spiritual typography. His first encounters with Yahweh began with the cloud - a visible, tangible manifestation of a divine presence that served as an initial gateway into the supernatural realm. This cloud, while mysterious, remained somewhat comprehensible. It represented the "outer chambers" of divine revelation, where God makes Himself known to those who seek Him.

This reveals that the progression from cloud to thick darkness isn't a movement away from divine light, but a journey into its source. The cloud serves as a preparatory realm, conditioning our spiritual senses for deeper encounters.

"Black clouds and deep darkness" points to layers of divine reality that become increasingly concentrated and intense. These layers correspond to different levels of divine wisdom, each more profound than the last.

THE FIRE WITHIN THE DARKNESS

The paradoxical combination of fire and darkness in **Deuteronomy 4:11** reveals another dimension of this spiritual progression. The fire "blazing to the very heavens" while coexisting with "black clouds and deep darkness" presents a divine contradiction.

This fire within darkness represents what we call "black fire" - a level of divine energy so intense that it appears as darkness. The thick darkness represents the superabundance of revelation around it.

This transformation is a fundamental shift in our capacity to perceive and interact with divine reality. The thick darkness becomes a womb of spiritual rebirth, being reformed according to higher patterns of divine wisdom.

The Hebrew term for this thick darkness, "araphel" (ערפל), carries profound significance. What appears as impenetrable darkness to our limited perception is actually an overwhelming abundance of divine light – so intense that our finite minds can only perceive it as darkness. Therefore, the treasures of darkness, the אוֹצָר חֹשֶׁךְ (ʾô·ṣār ḥō·šĕk), contain the highest mysteries of

God's nature. Journeying into this dense darkness is ascending to higher dimensions. Here lie the most precious divine secrets and the deepest treasures of spiritual wisdom.

This journey of ascension, from the initial encounters with divine presence to the profound depths of the thick darkness, is an invitation to move past surface experiences and dive into the realms where true transformation occurs. It challenges you to grow beyond your comfort zones, to embrace the purifying and transforming fires, to attune your spiritual ears to sounds of transition, and courageously step into the unknown and discover the greatest mysteries of God.

Genesis 1:2, which states, "The earth was without form, and void; and darkness was on the face of the deep. And the Spirit of God was hovering over the face of the waters."

This primordial darkness was actually a state of perfect potential, where all possibilities existed in perfect unity before differentiation. Therefore, entering the thick darkness brings us back to this original state of pure potential, a place where new realities are born. This primordial darkness, known in Hebrew as חֹשֶׁךְ (ḥō·šěḵ) entangled with "tehom" (the deep). Here we encounter gods and thrones - spiritual entities with responsibilities to govern realms and dimensions in the spirit.

When ascension leads you into the darkness, you enter a deep realm where you encounter entities known as elohims and angelic realms that surpass our understanding. We're entering a realm that's beyond our current capabilities, a place that has been off-limits to us until now. But as we progress in our ascension journey, similar to Moses who governed God's household, Jesus opens these doors and invites us to explore the profound depths of mystery.

This understanding transforms our reading of **Psalm 97:1-3**. By referring to clouds and thick darkness enveloping the Lord, the passage reveals a cosmic truth: the greatest mysteries are veiled within layers of obscurity. Just as the Zohar describes a place "concealed and known to none but the Holy One," these layers of darkness protect and preserve the most sacred revelations until we're prepared to receive them. The realm of darkness is pregnant with potential, waiting to birth new revelations.

Isaiah 45:3 NKJV

I will give you the treasures of darkness, And hidden riches of secret places, That you may know that I, the Lord, Who call you by your name, Am the God of Israel.

Isaiah 45:3 holds the sacred promise of concealed treasures nestled within secret chambers. These treasures, like blueprints, yearn for the revelation of sonship. Discovering these treasures reveals a majestic ascension, granting the power to behold, touch, and liberate what has long been concealed. The pursuit of these hidden wonders intricately intertwines with your very essence as an ascension matrix.

In **1 Kings 8:12**, we read, "Then Solomon said, The Lord has said that he would dwell in a dark cloud."

The darkness and cloud, points back to the beginning of creation referred to in Genesis. When God speaks about darkness, He is transporting your spirit back to the inception of creation, because His divine plan is to entangle your destiny with those primordial mysteries. As the "ב" - the point of release in creation, you channel divine purpose into existence. The realm of memory represents His awakening of your original existence, stirring the sound of your position to co-create with Him. The realm of memory comes alive, vibrating the ancient pages of your hidden scroll in Him, recollecting your purpose of divine union in Him.

Psalm 97:1-3, "The Lord reigns, let the earth be glad; let the distant shores rejoice. Clouds and thick darkness surround him; righteousness and justice are the foundation of his throne. Fire goes before him and consumes his foes on every side."

This passage paints a vivid picture of the Lord surrounded by clouds and thick darkness, with mysteries and secrets enveloping Him. It's a realm of divine governance, where righteousness and justice form the foundation of His throne.

That these realms encompass Him reveals that the realm of mystery is an extension of His glorious being. Wherever Yahweh's presence goes, mystery manifests and saturates the atmosphere with hidden treasures of darkness. As sons of the new creation, we navigate a life brimming with unfamiliarity, lacking any frame of reference for our ultimate destination. Unseen sights encompass us, unheard sounds, and the unexplored reverberates within our very beings. With Christ dwelling within you, that same cloud envelops you, infusing your destiny with enigmatic possibilities. It becomes the ultimate exhilarating journey to venture into the unknown, unlocking the potential within and transforming mystery into a tangible reality. God wrapping Himself in darkness becomes our own pattern. We, too, learn to wrap ourselves in these sacred mysteries, allowing them to transform us from within. This is what it means to truly govern in the spiritual realms: not standing outside the darkness in fear, but entering it with the confidence of those who understand its true nature.

Justin Paul Abraham: "I'd rather be inexperienced in the new than experienced in the old."

Embrace the uncertainty and give yourself the grace to stumble amidst the vast expanse of unexplored spiritual realms. Feel the tangibility of potential arrest you as you navigate through the landscapes of endless possibilities. Listen closely to the whispering of the heavens, carrying messages from unseen realms. Allow the thrill of the unknown to awaken your spiritual senses and guide you on this enlightening journey.

Psalms 19:1-2 TPT, "God's splendour is a tale that is told, written in the stars. Space itself speaks his story through the marvels of the heavens. His truth is on tour in the starry vault of the sky, showing his skill in creation's craftsmanship. Each day gushes out its message to the next, night by night whispering its knowledge to all."

Exodus 24:1, "Then the Lord said to Moses, 'Come up to the Lord, you and Aaron, Nadab and Abihu, and seventy of the elders of Israel. You are to worship at a distance, but Moses alone is to **approach** the Lord; the others must not come near. And the people may not come up with him.'"

In the Hebrew language, the word עֲלֵה (aleh) is used to express the concept of 'come up 'and suggests a sense of being aided in the ascent. The 70 elders mentioned here were crucial leaders who played a significant role in governing the Israelites. This also symbolises the divine governance and cosmic order, aligning with the concept of angelic collaboration and spiritual administration. Mystical writings point to the fact that the 70 represents the celestial order of cosmic governance. The number 70 corresponds to the numerical value of the Hebrew letter ע, which is associated with complete dimensional vision. To master the art of summoning and invoking angelic realms, you can call upon the angels specifically assigned to assist you in your administration and ascent. Moses, being a reflection of the higher realms, served as a shepherd who brought down supernal wisdom to guide the lower worlds. In this role, he was appointed over the forces below, much like a king appoints his trusted servant.

Jesus assigns heavenly beings to accompany you, and it is your responsibility to name them according to their function and provide them with instructions. The concept of naming angelic beings and aligning their roles corresponds to the alignment of divine letters, the Hebrew Letters, that govern creation. It is, however, important to start the process of establishing a council that will support you in your rule.

The elders were told to stay back, but Moses could 'approach'.

The Hebrew word implies a more active action than simply 'coming closer', it signifies 'stepping into'.

The focus is on unlocking the hidden treasures within yourself. When Christ is within you, the entire spiritual realm lives within you. Imagine that - your being contains the entire spiritual realm. Ascension is the pathway for you to explore, unlock, and unleash the ancient ways within you.

The 70 elders and Aaron were told to worship, show reverence, and bow down in the presence of Yahweh, but Moses received a special invitation to step into His presence. The significance lies in the fact that Yahweh perceived Moses as an embodiment of Himself. By understanding that Yahweh sees you as an embodiment of Himself, your authority and confidence will break through to higher dimensions. Moses ascended to the supernal realms, cleaving to the divine light.

"The elders remained at a distance, gazing at the radiance but not partaking of the inner mystery."

Exodus 7:1, where God says to Moses, "See, I have made you like God to Pharaoh, and your brother Aaron will be your prophet."

Yahweh tells Moses, "You are Me to Pharaoh." Moses truly embodies the full manifestation of God. This understanding has the incredible ability to transform your perception of your own potential. It opens your eyes to the countless opportunities that await you, the unique talents you possess, the uncharted worlds you can explore, and the profound impact you can have on different realms.

As you embrace your role as an Elohim, you step into a heightened awareness of your divine abilities and purpose. As a god, you recognise the limitless potential that flows through your bloodline, empowering you to summon and wield extraordinary forces. When summoned by God, the celestial beings in the spirit realm fall into a hushed silence, their gaze fixed upon you, eagerly awaiting your every word. His intention is for the spirit realm to acknowledge your presence and respond to your summons.

THE SAPPHIRE THRONE: GATEWAY TO DIVINE REVELATION

Exodus 24:9-11 "Moses and Aaron, Nadab and Abihu, and the seventy elders of Israel went up and saw את the God of Israel. Under his feet was something like a **pavement made of lapis lazuli**, as bright blue as the sky. But God did not raise his hand against these leaders of the Israelites; they saw את God, and they ate and drank."

The verse describes that "they saw." Between the word "saw" and "God," the את appears in the Hebrew Bible. The profound significance of the את (Aleph-Tav) continues to reveal layers of mystical understanding how the elders perceived the divine presence. The את, blending the Hebrew alphabet's first and last letters encapsulates completion. It acted as a cosmic lens through which elders perceived the multidimensional image and glory of God. Jewish mystics interpret את as a marker of divine presence, specifically pointing to the Messiah, who is the beginning and the end.

Moses's second ascension clearly opened new realms. Yahweh called Moses to enter a higher dimension than in his first ascension, for in those earlier scriptures, the את do not appear. Yet in this ascension, they do, unveiling the hidden mystery of Jesus in the Old Testament.

The את represents the complete spectrum of creation, from beginning to end. When placed between the verb "saw" ראה and "God" אלהים, it suggests that their vision penetrated through all layers of reality into mystical vision. The Aleph-Tav contains all 22 letters of the Hebrew alphabet, which, according to mystical teaching, are the building blocks of creation. This verse's use of "את" is significant, as it appears during a divine revelation. Therefore, the elders observed God as He manifested through the interconnected realms and dimensions of all creation's elements, like a prism, exploding justice and mercy, transcendence and immanence to comprehend divine unity through multiplicity. They saw through what the mystics call the "clear lens" (אספקלריה המאירה) (aspeklarya ha-me'irah), usually reserved for a prophetic vision of the highest order.

The unique vision via the את also served as a preparation for receiving the Torah, since the את encompassed all the letters

141

needed to deliver the Torah.

The elders, drinking and eating in His presence, immersed themselves in a timeless connection, experiencing fellowship with Him, the beginning and the end converging in the memory of their primordial state.

Sapphire, known as סַפִּיר, in this passage is the first occurrence of this word in the Hebrew Bible and plays a significant role in the throne room of God. It opens gateways to the divine message, allowing you to engage with the living Word and become vessels within vessels, wheels within wheels. As you are seated with Christ in heavenly realms, you position yourself within סַפִּיר. This sacred space enables you to tap into inter-dimensional abilities and witness the extraordinary manifestation of Yeshua. While everything in the Bible is of God, not everything of God is found within the Bible. Paul spoke from this profound place, and that is why Moses received the commandments on sapphire tablets. Within סַפִּיר lies the hidden secrets and mysteries of the divine word. This sheds light on why Yahweh reacted so strongly when Moses, in a fit of anger, shattered the tablets as they were pulsing with Yahweh's Word, a part of His divine throne, an extension of His being.

SAPPHIRE IS A DIMENSION OF THE KINGDOM.

In "The Legends of the Jews," Louis Ginzberg describes a profound mystery within Jewish mysticism: God took the tablets from His own throne, and these tablets of sapphire vibrated with the living Word of God, the commandments themselves. As Yahweh engraved His finger across the tablets, the Hebrew letters emerged, interweaving and combining to form His divine commandments.

The gematria for סַפִּיר is 350, with 8 symbolising Chet ח

entangled with the spirit of wisdom. As we engage with סַפִּיר, we will simultaneously experience the dance of creativity and wisdom. Embedded within סַפִּיר are secrets that pertain to the authority and governance of the sons.

According to the throne description of God, it is made of lapis lazuli or sapphire. This beautiful blue stone, adorned with golden flecks, holds much more than mere physical beauty - it encapsulates profound spiritual realities. Deep within the essence of sapphire, the very frequencies of the Word of God resonate. Each Hebrew letter intricately weaves together, forming a beautiful arc of connectivity. When two letters intersect, they establish a point of connection, giving rise to a portal or dimension. This interweaving of the divine word within lapis lazuli creates a mesmerising display of frequencies and colours, mirroring the magnificent rainbow that adorns God's heavenly throne room.

When you connect with lapis lazuli during your spiritual journey, realise that it's significance goes beyond a mere gemstone. This precious sapphire intricately links to angelic realms and carries the divine Word of God within its essence. Jeremiah had a deep understanding of this truth when he penned the words in **Jeremiah 14:21**, pleading, "Please do not despise us for the sake of Your name; do not dishonour Your glorious throne. Remember Your covenant with us and do not break it." The sapphire throne, representing the very embodiment of God's Word, symbolises His unwavering commitment to honour His name and protect the sanctity of His throne.

In **Revelation 4:3**, it is written, "And the one seated there had the appearance of jasper and ruby. A rainbow, shining like an emerald, encircled the throne."

This passage symbolises the intertwining of the seven spirits of God with lapis lazuli. When you encounter lapis lazuli or the sapphire floor during your spiritual journey, it signifies a profound connection with the word of God. When God places you on the sapphire, He is inviting you to delve deeper into His word and engage with it on a more profound level.

Ezekiel 1:26 confirms this imagery: "Above the vault over their heads was what looked like a throne of lapis lazuli, and high above on the throne was a figure like that of a man."

This sapphire throne is accompanied by remarkable sights, as described in **Revelation 4:4-6**: "Surrounding the throne were twenty-four other thrones, and seated on them were twenty-four elders. They were dressed in white and had crowns of gold on their heads. From the throne came flashes of lightning, rumblings and peals of thunder. In front of the throne, seven lamps were blazing. These are the seven spirits of God. Also, in front of the throne there was what looked like a sea of glass, clear as crystal. In the centre, around the throne, were four living creatures, and they were covered with eyes, in front and in back."

As Moses gazed upon Yahweh standing on the sapphire floor, he witnessed Hebrew letters gracefully dancing, infusing life into the sapphire itself. He observed the four living creatures encircling the majestic throne, which seemed to rise from the very essence of the sapphire, while simultaneously the sapphire appeared to emerge from the throne, and the throne from God Himself. It became clear that the throne and God were inseparable, forever intertwined as one in their divine nature.

Colossians 3:1–2 NIV, "Since then, you have been raised with Christ, set your hearts on things above, where Christ is, seated at the right hand of God. Set your minds on things above, not on earthly things."

The Mirror Bible describes the above verse as: "See yourselves co-raised with Christ! Now ponder with persuasion the consequence of your co-inclusion in Him. Relocate yourselves mentally! Engage your thoughts with throne room realities where you are co-seated with Christ in the executive authority of God's right hand. Become affectionately acquainted with throne room thoughts will keep you from being distracted again by the earthly."

As you ascend, ask the Father to ascend you into the sapphire of His throne, where He will unveil His revelations to you. The throne room, known as the gyroscope of creation, imparts motion to all. It serves as the central point around which everything revolves. Representing divine government and order, the headquarters of every divine plan.

Whenever sapphire appears in your ascension, it hints at the unfolding of significant events. It shows that the government of heaven has revealed itself on your mountain. During such moments, Yahweh desires to release something of great importance into your environment, entrusting you to be a steward of its mysteries. The interweaving of Hebrew letters, words, and the seven spirits of God generates a spiritual intensity with parallel.

On this journey of ascension, you embark by experiencing the divine presence, which eventually guides you to the profound depths of the sapphire throne. It is an invitation to go beyond surface experiences and dive into the realms where true transformation takes place. This journey challenges you to expand your boundaries, to embrace the purifying and transforming fires of divine encounter, and to attune your spiritual senses to the frequencies of heaven. It urges you to step courageously into the unknown, where your discovery of the greatest mysteries of God awaits.

As we ascend, we are not mere observers, but rather active participants in the divine governance of creation. Our calling is to engage with the sapphire throne, interpret the dance of Hebrew letters, commune with the living creatures, and steward the mysteries that are being released from the depths of Tehom. This is the elevated purpose of the sons of God - not merely to visit these realms, but to govern from them and bring the realities of heaven into the contexts of earth.

In this transformative journey of ascension, we align ourselves to perceive through the divine lens - as an Elohim, as co-creators, as entrusted bearers of the enigmatic kingdom's wisdom. It is a summons to mature beyond rudimentary teachings and embrace our celestial essence completely. As we embark on this ancient path, we become conduits of celestial revelations, gracefully tending to the hidden treasures and secrets that God eagerly yearns to unleash upon creation.

Quieting our minds and opening our spirits to the mysteries that await in the sapphire throne room is the womb of adventure. Through these encounters, we not only discover more of Yahweh but also uncover more of our true selves in Him. This journey of ascension takes us deep into the heart of God, where our divine purpose becomes fully realised and we find our true selves.

"In stillness, we find the gateway to boundless exploration."

THE REALM OF BECOMING

In **Exodus 24:12**, the Lord said to Moses, "**Come up to Me** on the mountain and stay there, and I will give you the tablets of stone with the law and commandments I have written for their instruction." The seventy elders, Aaron, and his sons were to stay behind.

Note it was Yahweh (the LORD) who spoke, not Elohim (God).

Yahweh said to Moses, "Come up to Me on the mountain and stay here." He called Moses into a higher dimension than where Aaron, his sons, and the seventy elders remained.

In the realm of ascension, there is a place where fellowship and communion intertwine, enveloped by His presence. It is a sanctuary of revelation, where the veils of mystery lift, revealing profound revelations. In this sacred space, His presence quickens your spirit and invites you to experience the profound mysteries awaiting in the realm of communion.

When Yahweh says, "come up to Me," the Hebrew describes it as "entering inside of Me." He told Aaron and the seventy elders to stay where they were, but He commanded Moses to ascend INTO Him. After instructing Moses to ascend inside of Him, He instructed everyone else to stay put. Positioned in the place where God called him to, Moses stepped into the very essence of what he had witnessed at the burning bush.

At the burning bush, Moses had his first encounter with the Presence, but God did not allow him to draw near. Here, however, God allowed him to ascend, to step into His very essence and to remain in I AM WHO I AM.

The true depth of ascension becomes apparent when you embrace its practice, as Jesus unlocks the potential within your DNA for growth and change, the revelation of becoming. Religion mocks, "Who do you think you are?" Jesus declares, "I know who you are."

'Stay behind' is the Hebrew word היה and is defined as" to become" as transitioning into a state of being. It is also the root for אֶהְיֶה אֲשֶׁר אֶהְיֶה.. I AM WHO I AM.

Thus, Yahweh is saying, "Position yourself, step into Me and entangle my being, become I AM WHO I AM." This was the

THE REALM OF BECOMING

fulfilment of what Moses first encountered at the burning bush. Some Rabbinical and Jewish sources would not support the idea of stepping in and become one, but our approach remains Christ centred and the fulfilment we experience from the finished work of the cross.

"You must remove your shoes and not come close, for where you stand is holy ground."

Yet when Moses ascended the mountain the second time, God spoke to him, saying, "Step into Me. When you step into Me, you can enter into 'I AM WHO I AM' and experience the fullness. You embody Me."

THE SONS OF WONDER

Exodus 24:12 NIV The Lord said to Moses, "Come up to me on the mountain and stay here, and I will give you את the tablets of **stone** with the law and commandments I have written for their instruction."

Note how Yahweh first positioned Moses? Between the words "give you" and "tablets of stone," we have the את. He says, "I will give you..." (from the beginning א to the end ת) the inscription upon these tablets of stone, which is the very embodiment of the Word, Yeshua. The את carries the mysteries of creation and the manifestation of the wonders within Yeshua.

The Hebrew word for "stone" is אבן (even)—composed of א (Aleph), ב (Bet), and נ (Nun). Grammatically, the ב is pronounced as "v" rather than "b." This is intimately connected to the Hebrew word בן (ben), meaning "son." As Scripture declares in First Peter, you are living stones. By giving Moses the stones, Yahweh imparted the essence of Moses as a living stone, a divine entanglement and arcing of mandates.

The DNA within the tablets intertwined with Moses's own DNA as a Son of God—Ben intertwining with Ben—son and stone, living stones, transforming into sons of wonder.

This bears profound significance, for Scripture proclaims: "I will write the laws upon your hearts." You are stones, you are tablets. If you are the sapphire stone, you are part of Yahweh Himself—an emanation from His being. You are a significant presence within God's throne, personifying His Word in a living form.

Ascension and meditation activation for the realm of the sons of wonder is available at the end of the book.

THE DIMENSIONS OF GLORY

In **Exodus 24:13**, we read: "Then Moses set out with Joshua his aide, and Moses went up on the mountain of God." Verse 15 continues: "When Moses went up on the mountain, the cloud covered it, and the **glory** of the LORD settled on Mount Sinai. For six days, the cloud את covered the mountain, and on the seventh day the LORD called to Moses from within the cloud."

Again, after scripture mentions "the cloud covered," the את appears. The את is a reminder of the higher realm Moses was engaging.

When you experience the magnificence of the glory of Yahweh's presence during ascension, note these 4 dimensions:

Kavod כָּבוֹד is the Hebrew word for '**glory**' and embodies four dimensions in this realm.

The cloud served as a garment for divine glory, through which Moses passed through multiple "veils" to unlock divine communion. The presence of את signals the bridge between transcendent and immanent divine presence. This marking shows the higher realm Moses was engaging, transitioning between human perception and divine reality.

When experiencing the magnificence of Yahweh's presence during ascension, we identify **four dimensions of glory (כָּבוֹד - kavod):**

1. The Splendour of Yahweh

The dimension we are discussing here is known as "the illuminating mirror," representing pure radiant beauty that is directly connected to the presence of God. Psalm 145:5 proclaims, "They speak of the glorious splendour of Your majesty, and I will meditate on Your wonderful works." In the literature of Ma'aseh Merkavah, this splendour is described as being so powerful that even the highest angels need to veil themselves in its presence.

2. The Glory of God as Honour

The כָּבוֹד (kavod) in its honour aspect embodies the "depth of beginning and the depth of the end." This relates to the esteem and reverence of Yahweh's nature and essence. As taught by Rabbi Isaac Luria, this divine dimension acts as a vessel, delicately receiving and channeling higher light into the lower realms. Lower doesn't necessarily mean a lesser, but a progression of unfolding. Its gentle embrace ensures the recipients are not overwhelmed, allowing them to bask in the magnificence.

3. The Wealth of His Presence

Glory, connected to divine abundance, shows that כָּבוֹד holds all forms of spiritual and material wealth. It is "the treasury of all treasuries" from which all blessings flow. While this encompasses material riches, it carries broader significance as spiritual abundance. When we step into Yahweh's glory, as Rabbi Moses Cordovero explains in Pardes Rimonim, we access what he calls "the divine economy," through which spiritual riches flow downward through increasingly dense levels of manifestation.

4. The Demonstration of His Power

The strong hand and outstretched arm manifesting as tangible demonstrations of His divine authority through miracles, signs, and wonders.

These four dimensions are not separate but are the four faces of the same light. They are the four levels of spiritual perception, from the awareness of divine presence to the direct experience of divine power. As Moses experienced on Sinai, these dimensions form a constant flow through which divine presence maintains and elevates creation.

When we encounter these dimensions of glory, we are being invited into a journey of moving through layers of divine presence, with each layer unveiling a more profound aspect of Yahweh's manifest glory. Each dimension of glory becomes a pathway to a more profound connection with Yahweh.

THE CHANNEL OF DIVINE PERFECTION

Exodus 24:15-16, it states the Lord called Moses up, and Moses dwelt in Yahweh's presence for **six** days. On the **seventh** day, God spoke to him.

This scripture unfolds with mystical undertones, inviting contemplation on the deeper symbolic layers of Moses 'six-day dwelling in Yahweh's presence and the climactic revelation on the seventh day. The Hebrew letters vav (ו) and zayin (ז), with their numerical and spiritual significances, anchor this passage within the framework of divine mysteries, particularly through their connection to creation, identity, and ascension.

THE SIGNIFICANCE OF VAV (ו): CONNECTION AND DNA

The letter ו, corresponding to the numerical value six, is often referred to as the "connector" in Hebrew mysticism. Grammatically, it serves as a conjunction, linking words, ideas, and phrases. Spiritually, it represents the binding force that unites heaven and earth. The six days Moses spent in Yahweh's presence symbolise a process of divine entanglement—God weaving His essence, or "divine DNA," into Moses.

In mystical thought, ו is associated with the six dimensions of physical reality (north, south, east, west, above, and below) and the six days of creation. These six days of Moses' dwelling signify the work of transformation, where the raw material of Moses' being is refined and aligned with divine purpose. Just as DNA serves as the blueprint for physical life, the divine ו signifies a spiritual blueprint, encoding Moses with the mysteries of divine ascension and kingship.

This "spiritual DNA entanglement" echoes the concept of tzelem Elohim (the image of God). By dwelling in Yahweh's presence, Moses is progressively transformed into a vessel capable of embodying God's authority and glory, a realm that brought order to chaos, culminating in the sanctity of the seventh day. Similarly, during these six days, Moses is being re-ordered and prepared for the revelation to come, a divine download.

The Hebrew word (סֻלָּם) "sullām", which translates to "ladder" or "stairway" in English, is most famously used in the book of Genesis (28:12) in relation to Jacob's dream. In this dream, Jacob sees a (סֻלָּם) "sullām" extending from earth to heaven, with angels ascending and descending upon it. Mysticism widely interprets this vision as spiritual ascension, emphasising the connection between the person as a Vav ו and the spiritual realms.

The 'stairway' in **Genesis 28:12**, known as "sullam" (סלם) in Hebrew, comes from the word "salal" סלל, meaning "**to build up.**" סלל is also connected to קלל, our 3rd ascension word. The Hebrew word סָלַל is a verb that is typically translated as **"to lift up", "to exalt", "to cast up", "to heap", or "to pile up"**. It is often used in the context of preparing a road or a way, specifically people using it to remove obstacles or make a path smoother or more passable. This usage can be seen in the Book of **Isaiah 40:4**" Every valley shall be lifted up (sā·lăl), and every mountain and hill be made low; the uneven ground shall become level, and the rough places a plain." In this verse, the metaphorical use of sā·lăl serves the purpose of paving a divine path for God's arrival. While you don't need to make preparations for any arrivals since Christ lives within you, סלל symbolises an ascension that readies you for the divine manifestations of Jesus' image within you.

What makes this word סלל intriguing, is that it is the only Hebrew term used to describe an ascending structure, not a physical staircase, but a spiritual one. By ascending this spiritual structure, we engage in the process of constructing a manifest spiritual reality that you are an ascension channel, the divine ו.

Once we have unlocked and inhabited these realms, we not only experience them but also become one with them. Ascension is a process of rising through multiple interconnected spiritual planes.

Consider the Scripture, "Be holy because I am holy." However, this isn't just a command for action; rather, it serves as an invitation into a state of being. By embracing this invitation, you position yourself within the divine reality. Ascension plays a crucial role in unlocking the consciousness of being, leading to a state of rest and peace in divine shalom. Ascension doesn't accomplish peace as much as it settles you in that realm. Jesus is the prince of peace, and the ascension structure of סלל entangles the realms of shalom, revealing dimensions of the seventh day. As we continue to grow and develop, our awareness and consciousness expand. Once we have unlocked these realms, we learn the state of being.

In our ascension practice, Yahweh continues to unlock revelations. The entire ascension process serves to unlock remembrance, effectively restoring us to our original position, state, manifestation, and authority.

Matthew 7:7 tells us, "Ask and it will be given to you; seek and you will find." This is ascension. "Knock and the door will be opened to you." Ascension manifested.

THE REVELATION OF ZAYIN (ז): COMPLETION AND KINGSHIP

The seventh day introduces the letter zayin ז, which has a numerical value of seven and is deeply connected to the concepts of rest, completion, and kingship. Where vav is a straight line representing connection, zayin is a crowned vav, signifying the elevation of connection into sovereignty. Mystically, the seventh day represents a culmination—a moment when divine potential reaches fruition.

On this day, God spoke to Moses, not as to a servant, but to a king, affirming his role as an Elohim, a divinely authorised ruler. The seventh day is permeated with rest, a state of completeness and readiness for a divine purpose. This rest mirrors the Sabbath, where creation pauses to reflect divine perfection.

The connection between zayin and kingship is emphasised by its symbolic association with the sword. While it represents rest, zayin also embodies the readiness to wield divine authority in alignment with God's will. The seventh-day communication between God and Moses signifies both a culmination and a confirmation of Moses' readiness to lead, govern, and be God's divine channel.

The interplay of ı and т reflects the movement between the physical and the spiritual, the temporal and the eternal. In these six days, Moses ascends through the spiritual realms, progressively shedding layers of his limited human identity and ascending into his divine potential. Ascension, in this context, is not merely an external event but an internal unveiling of the mysteries encoded within him.

Each day of Moses' dwelling corresponds to a step on the "staircase of ascension," with vav serving as the structural rungs and zayin marking the transition to the final, crowned state. This journey mirrors the process of spiritual growth, moving through the phases of transformation until you are ready to fully receive and act upon divine revelation.

When the seventh day arrives, Yahweh speaks, affirming Moses' rulership. This interaction emphasises that divine authority is not imposed, but awakened. By acknowledging Moses as an Elohim, God reveals that Moses' identity was quickened through transformation. No longer just a servant, Moses' identity embodies the divine image. He is entrusted with the authority to govern, lead, and act as a mediator between heaven and earth, divinely positioned for the revelation of the sapphire tablets. In Exodus 24:15-16, this passage encapsulates a profound mystical journey, where the vav symbolises the process of connection and transformation, and the т heralds the fulfilment of divine purpose. Together, they unveil the deeper truth that ascension is both a return to one's divine origins and a stepping into one's rightful authority as a co-creator with God.

"Rest mirrors the Sabbath, where creation pauses to reflect divine perfection."

MYSTERY OF THE 40 DAYS AND 40 NIGHTS

Exodus 24:17–18 NIV "To the Israelites, the glory of the Lord looked like a consuming fire on top of the mountain. Then Moses entered the cloud as he went on up the mountain. And he **stayed** on the mountain **forty** days and forty nights."

When Moses ascended Mount Sinai, he reached a state

of perfect harmony with infinite light. The Hebrew term used to describe his "stay" on the mountain—אֶהְיֶה ('ĕh·yĕ(h))—is derived from the same root as God's self-revelation: "I AM WHO I AM." This linguistic link implies that Moses's forty-day experience went beyond mere physical presence; it embodied a profound spiritual merging with the very essence of God.

The glory of the Lord appeared as a "consuming fire" (Exodus 24:17), symbolising the transformative power of divine presence. According to Rabbi Abraham Abulafia's teachings, this encounter started a profound spiritual transformation where the boundaries between human consciousness and divine awareness dissolved. The fire represented not destruction but transformation, a process of spiritual refinement that allowed Moses to transcend physical limitations. That's the beauty of ascension...LIMITLESS POSSIBILITIES!

The number forty corresponding to the Hebrew letter מ (mem). מ represents water, both physical and spiritual, and serves as a gateway to primordial wisdom. The forty-day period represents a complete cycle of transformation, much like the forty weeks of human pregnancy or the forty years of wilderness wandering.

This period divides into forty days and forty nights, representing the dual nature of spiritual reality.

- The forty days symbolise the exploration of mayim elyonim (upper waters), associated with the open mem (מ)

- The forty nights correspond to the mayim tachtonim (lower waters), represented by the closed mem sofit (ם)

The Zohar teaches that the separation of the upper and lower waters in Genesis reflects a cosmic reality that Moses encountered during his ascent up the mountain. This separation, however, is not meant to maintain division, but to create a sacred union. Moses's forty-day experience symbolised the harmonious integration of these waters, a mystical merging of heavenly and earthly, masculine and feminine energies. Since Moses's name begins with מ, it serves as the gateway for his identity to connect with heaven's blueprint, awakening his ancient scroll as a guardian of the mysteries. It is the hidden and potential merging that leads to the divine revelation... Moses, the one who unveils.

During the forty days, his transformation occurred, enabling him to serve as a living bridge connecting these realms. His encounter with divine union became the model for all subsequent spiritual ascension, revealing the capacity of human consciousness to harmonise with divine will and manifest spiritual realities. This mystical process intertwines human and divine essence, as prolonged immersion in the divine presence reshapes human consciousness, enabling it to mirror the divine reality. "Christ in you, the hope of glory" represents the immense potential within you, with ascension as the key to unlock its manifestation. Rabbi Isaac Luria describes this process as a spiritual "imprinting," where divine patterns become encoded in human awareness. The forty-day period provided the duration for this transformation to complete itself.

During his forty-day experience, Moses delved into what mystical texts refer to as the "matrix of creation" - a co-creating space where divine will materialises into physical reality. The letter mem symbolises this matrix, representing the belly or womb. This period witnessed Moses' spiritual development, characterised by a transformation of his consciousness to align with the patterns of the divine.

The transformation resulted in Moses gaining the ability to receive and transmit the Torah. The tablets he brought down from the mountain represented the law, but also embodied divine wisdom in a physical form. These two tablets serve as a reflection of the duality present in the upper and lower waters, heaven and earth, and masculine and feminine aspects, all harmoniously united through the transformative power of forty.

The union of upper and lower waters speaks to integrating spiritual insight with practical action. The symbol מ serves as a reminder that all creation emerges from and returns to divine unity. This mysterious concept emphasises the importance of true spiritual transformation. It highlights the need to practice ascension, during which we learn to unite heaven and earth, spirit and matter. By doing so, we unlock a deeper consciousness of our co-creating ability.

Exodus 24:18 "Then Moses entered the cloud as he went up the mountain, and he stayed on the mountain forty days ו and forty nights." The **New King James Version** states: "So Moses went into the midst of the cloud and went up into the mountain. And Moses was on the mountain for forty days and forty nights. So the Lord called from within the cloud. And Moses entered."

Between "forty days" and "forty nights" appears the Hebrew letter ו (vav). The construction would appear as מ-ו-מ (mem-vav-mem), with the final mem closing the word. Meaning Moses entangled the mirror dimensions of the mysteries of God's Kingdom.

The first ו in Scripture appears in **Genesis 1:1** between heaven and earth. The position of the ו in Genesis supports Moses' position to transfer from the heavenly to the earthly realm.

"In the realm of mystery stewardship, God entrusts you with a revelation to nurture. It is within your power and responsibility to shape how this revelation manifests itself on earth."

As the vav, the number six, representing humanity, you are the connection point, allowing others to experience the supernatural through their encounters with you. You are the conductor and relay of mysteries.

Consider the spiritual highway you embody and your capacity to influence atmospheres wherever you go—in shopping malls, workplaces, everywhere. As earlier mentioned, I grammatically functions as a conversive prefix. That means it transforms verbs from the past to future tense and vice versa. This suggests functioning beyond space-time constraints. Time serves you as you exist "in the above."

Ironically, as I searched for a Hebrew word combining mem, vav, and mem מום, I stumbled upon one that, initially, left me disappointed. In Hebrew, this word means "spot" or "blemish." However, through meditation, I came to understand its profound connection to our ascension in Jesus. It is clear you cannot engage the spirit realm outside the cross. This word serves as a revelation that ascension exists solely in Christ. While New Age practitioners and occultists may attempt similar practices, they are actually engaging with different realms, opening their spirits to influences that are not Christ centred.

Leviticus 21:23: "Yet because of his defect, he must not go near the curtain or approach the altar and so desecrate my sanctuary. I am the LORD who makes them holy."

This same word for 'defect,' מום appears in **Song of Solomon 4:7**: "You are all fair, my love, and there is no 'spot' in you." In Christ, as Song of Songs reveals through its King, we stand in a perfect position to ascend and engage the heavenlies.

Let us understand: ascension is fundamentally a Christ centred practice—Sons of God practice ascension. That the New Age and occult have adopted similar practices leads some to claim mistakenly that we're engaging in their rituals. How often did Yahweh call Moses up? How often did He instruct John to "come up"? His constant invitation beckons you to ascend, to uncover and declare your true position. You are the intersection where the heavens and earth collide, giving rise to awe-inspiring and enigmatic wonders.

Ascension activation over n and the waters available at the end of the book

MYSTERY OF THE PILLAR CLOUD AND ASCENSION GATES

Exodus 33:8–11 NIV "And whenever Moses went out to the tent, all the people rose and stood at the entrances to their tents, watching Moses until he entered the tent. As Moses went into the tent, the **pillar of cloud** would come down and stay at the entrance, while the Lord spoke with Moses. Whenever the people saw the pillar of cloud standing at the entrance to the tent, they all stood and worshiped, each at the entrance to their tent. The Lord would speak to Moses face to face, as one speaks to a friend. Then Moses would return to the camp, but his young aide Joshua, son of Nun, did not leave the tent."

Though Moses wasn't physically up the mountain, God created an ascended state by causing the pillar to come down over the tent, serving as a portal of ascension. This remarkable sight led the people to worship, each from their tent's entrance.

It was during this time Yahweh spoke to Moses face to face, as one would speak to a friend. While Moses would eventually return to the camp, his aide Joshua, son of Nun, remained in the tent. This foreshadowed the permanently ascended state we have in Christ.

Joshua represents Jesus. With Christ dwelling within us, we never leave the tent, nor do we descend the mountain or forsake our ascended state. By practising ascension, we unlock a heightened awareness of our seated position with Christ in heavenly realms. As we continue to ascend, our understanding of these realms deepens, and we gain greater insight into what Jesus unveils for our active participation.

The pillar of cloud at the tent's entrance, a literal column connecting above and below, creating space for movement between realms. In Hebrew, this pillar עַמּוּד (ʿăm·mûḏ), depicts a mass of water particles, a watery atmosphere that reveals the mysteries of His image. Moses, as the I DNA ladder, could step in and engage in this dimensional shift.

Regarding portals and gateways—the Hebrew word "petach" פתח means door, opening, portal. With different vowel points פֶּ·תַח "pē·tăḥ", these same letters convey 'revelation'. When Yeshua declares, "I am the door," He speaks of paths where we enter and exit.

Jeremiah 17:19 illustrates this: This is what the Lord said to me: "Go and stand at the gate of the People, through which the kings of Judah go in and out; stand also at all the other gates of Jerusalem. Say to them, "Hear the word of the Lord, you kings of Judah and all the people of Judah and everyone living in Jerusalem who come through these gates."

Jerusalem's physical gates served as a reflection of the operations in the spiritual realm. It was at these gates where courts, judgments, and royal decrees took place. Now, in our journey of ascension, Yeshua becomes our gate, surrounded by entities who assist us along the way.

As Sons of God, we hold the authority to issue mandates at these gates. This concept is beautifully captured in **Revelation 3:20**, where it states, "Behold, I stand at the door and knock. If anyone hears My voice and opens the door, I will come in and dine with him, and he with Me."

The power to choose remains with us, making the process of ascension even more essential. The essence of the situation revolves around making a choice. Choices are catalysts to birth new creations. As we entangle, there is a release that takes place because we choose. Therefore, the idea of portals, gateways, and passages between dimensions comes into play. By deciding to open our minds and ascend, we not only deepen our connection with spirituality, but also play a crucial role in our maturity. Consider the imagery of Jacob's ladder in

Genesis 28:12 NIV "He had a dream in which he saw a stairway resting on the earth, with its top reaching to heaven, and the angels of God were ascending and descending on it."

With Christ living in you, you become the origin of spiritual ascension.

GATEWAYS OF ASCENSION: THE MYSTICAL DUALITY OF פֶּתַח (PETACH) AND דֶּלֶת (DALET):

In the landscape of Hebrew mysticism, the terms פֶּתַח (*Petach*) and דֶּלֶת (*Dalet*) serve as archetypes for spiritual gateways. While both convey the imagery of doors and portals, their mystical significance diverges, representing different aspects of access and revelation. These two portals, one dynamic and transformative, the other humble and invitational, illuminate distinct stages in the son's journey of ascension.

PETACH: THE GATEWAY OF REVELATION

The Hebrew word פֶּתַח (Petach) translates to **"portal," "opening," or "gateway."** Rooted in פתח, meaning "to open" or "to unveil,". Petach is an active threshold, a space that bridges the finite and the infinite. It calls you to step forward, engaging in a transformative act that unveils hidden mysteries.

Petach is the epitome of *revelation and transformation*. It represents the critical moment where the unformed intersects with the divine. Unlike a static doorway, it is alive with potential, inviting engagement and decision, symbolising a transition into new realms of understanding.

The gematria of פתח is 488 which deepens its mystical significance. This numerical value connects Petach to חפת (Chafat), the same gematria or numerical value, and means **"to wrap" or "to bind"**. Here, פֶּתַח wrapped you in mystery and חפת binds secrets to your mantle.

Genesis 4:7, God warns Cain: *"If you do well, will you not be accepted? And if you do not do well, sin lies at the door (פֶּתַח)."*

Here, Petach represents a pivotal choice, a gateway to either righteousness or sin. It is both an opportunity and a challenge, reflecting the duality of free will. Mystical writings describes the Shekhinah, or Divine Presence, standing at the Petach, waiting to be engaged. This paints Petach as a space where divine energy becomes accessible but only through human action.

Petach is essential for those who are prepared to embrace spiritual revelation. It symbolises the stage of ascension where you actively step into unknown dimensions, unveiling mysteries and nurture transformation. It is the gateway of courage and initiative, where momentum and choice define progress.

DALET: THE DOOR OF HUMILITY AND INVITATION

In contrast to Petach, דָּלֶת (Dalet) conveys a quieter, more gentle gateway. Translated as **"door,"** Dalet evokes the imagery of a threshold that waits to be opened. Its root, דל (dal), means **"poor" or "lowly,"** linking Dalet ד to humility and readiness. Where Petach stirs movement, Dalet invites stillness and surrender. My precious buddy, Justin Paul Abraham constantly reminds, that through ד, the door is in the floor.

Dalet reflects *humility, servitude, and divine invitation*. It is a door that patiently awaits engagement, embodying the quiet readiness to receive divine influence. The act of opening Dalet is one of submission, an acknowledgment of the son's dependence on divine grace embodied in Jesus.

When you reverse דלת to תלד you get the phrase **'she will give birth'.**

Genesis 17:16 "I will bless her, and she will give birth to a son."

The door of Dalet holds fulfilled promises.

Revelation 3:20, Christ proclaims: *"Behold, I stand at the door (דָּלֶת) and knock. If anyone hears My voice and opens the door, I will come in."*

This passage illustrates Dalet as an intimate point of invitation, where divine communion becomes possible for those willing to open their hearts. Mystical teachings reveal that Dalet ד is the conduit for blessings, but these blessings depend on human willingness to respond. Dalet embodies the threshold of readiness, the moment of choice to embrace divine connection.

Dalet is significant for sons to entangle humility and its divine influence. It represents the stage of ascension marked by quiet surrender and intimate communion, where you become a channel for divine grace.

INTERPLAY BETWEEN PETACH AND DALET:

Petach and Dalet, though distinct, are interconnected in the journey of spiritual ascent.

Petach quickens your boldness, to step into divine revelation. Dalet, invites stillness and humility, a readiness to receive the divine knock. Together, they form complementary gateways of the spiritual journey, reflecting both the dynamic and receptive dimensions of ascension.

PETACH AND DALET ILLUMINATE DIFFERENT PATHWAYS OF GROWTH:

These gateways are not mutually exclusive but cyclical, guiding you through an evolving relationship with Jesus. Yeshua's declaration in **John 10:7-9**, "I am the door," encompasses both Petach and Dalet. He is the active portal through which mysteries are unveiled and the humble door through which blessings flow.

In their interplay, Petach and Dalet reveal the essence of ascension: a balance between momentum and stillness, action and receptivity. Together, they lead the sons toward transformation and deeper union in Yahweh.

THE MYSTERY OF GOODNESS AND CROSSING OVER

Exodus 33:18–19 NIV Then Moses said to him, "If your Presence does not go with us, do not send us up from here. 16 How will anyone know that you are pleased with me and with your people unless you go with us? What else will distinguish me and your people from all the other people on the face of the earth?" 17 And the Lord said to Moses, "I will do the very thing you have asked, because I am pleased with you and I know you by name." 18 Then Moses said, "Now show me your **glory**." 19 And the Lord said, "I will cause all my **goodness** to **pass in front of you**, and I will **proclaim** my name, the Lord, in your presence. I will have mercy on whom I will have mercy, and I will have compassion on whom I will have compassion. 20 But," he said, "you cannot see my face, for no one may see me and live."

This passage initially puzzled me. Moses, having already experienced the glory cloud, the pillar of darkness, the very face of Yahweh atop the mountain, asks to see His glory, and to top it off, wasn't allowed to see God's face.

The Hebrew word for glory is כָּבוֹד (kavod)—splendour, the manifestation of divine power. Such glory in its fullness would obliterate anything in its presence. Glory manifests visually and experientially, which Moses sought. Is that not the glory he experienced on top of the mountain? Clearly, there was more.

Yahweh responded with: "I will cause my goodness to go before you." This statement is significant because it reveals the Hebrew word for "I will cause" as עָבַר (ʿā·ḇǎr), which means to **'crossover'** and is derived from the root word עבר, meaning **'Hebrew'**. Interestingly, it also carries the meaning of 'forgive'. By using this word, Yahweh was speaking directly into Moses's DNA and his identity as a Hebrew, establishing the powerful connection between the crossover of goodness through forgiveness and the ultimate manifestation of glory.

The Hebrew distinction between glory, known as כָּבוֹד (kavod), and goodness, referred to as טוב (ṭûḇ), has significance. While glory serves as a manifestation of God's power, goodness showcases His beauty and purity. This allows us to experience His holiness without being overwhelmed by the destructive force of His power.

When Scripture says, "pass in front of you," it uses פָּנֶה (paneh) face, a face-to-face interaction. As the goodness passed before Moses, it was the goodness and purity of Yahweh. They had a face-to-face interaction, entangling the divine nature of their connection.

I will 'proclaim 'My name is the word קָרָא (qara)—the same word used when God 'called 'Moses. This calling summoned him into divine presence, announced his status as a Son of God, invoked blessing over Moses as Elohim, and erupted worship. So He will proclaim his name in Moses 'face.

In this encounter, we witness the delicate dance between power and presence, between glory and goodness, that forms a foundation of mystical thought. Moses's request to see God's glory (kavod) reveals a mystery that there are always deeper levels of divine revelation and untold secrets, there is no end, and each revelation only hints at greater depths beyond.

By using עָבַר ('ā·ḇǎr), God speaks not just to Moses but through him, encoding the essence of primordial identity—the eternal crossover. This linguistic bridge connects the physical act of crossing over with the spiritual act of transformation.

The interplay between כָּבוֹד (kavod) and טוּב (ṭûḇ) reveals a mystical truth: that God's ultimate glory is most perfectly manifested not in overwhelming power, but in the intimate experience of divine goodness, God's self-contraction creates space for human encounter. His goodness is void of any performance, worthiness or qualification. It's the free gift of forgiveness we have in Jesus. The face-to-face (פָּנֶה/paneh) interaction echoes the mystical, where divine and human meet in transformative communion, the realm of completeness.

The proclamation (קָרָא/qara) of the divine name becomes not just an announcement, but an invitation into divine reality itself.

Like the mystics who saw the Hebrew letters as channels of divine energy, each pronunciation of the name creates a portal through which divine presence flows into human experience.

Sefer HaBahir: "The crossing over of light is the secret of creation: a movement from concealment to manifestation."

As the Jewish mystic Abraham Joshua Heschel once wrote: "The highest peak of spiritual living is not reaching out to God in prayer; it is letting God's divine goodness flow through you." In this moment with Moses, we see the blueprint for all mystical encounters—where glory becomes goodness, where power becomes presence, and where the infinite God makes himself intimately known through human experience.

In the ancient wisdom of the mystics lies a transformative truth - we exist simultaneously in multiple realms, with the power to traverse the veils between them. This art of crossing over, embedded in the Hebrew word (ʿā·ḇǎr)עָבַר, speaks to humanity's mystical capacity to bridge heaven and earth, matter and spirit, the finite and infinite, and the alchemy of combining.

Like water flowing between vessels, divine light seeks channels through which to pour into our world. The heart of the righteous becomes that vessel - not a passive container, but an active transformer of celestial energies. When we align our inner compass with divine purpose, we become living bridges, holy crossroads where the eternal collapses into the physical.

Transformation is not only about personal elevation, but about becoming a living portal through which divine goodness flows into a world thirsting for light where heaven and earth kiss. In every moment of prayer, meditation, or compassionate action, we take part in this cosmic crossing over, this holy alchemy where human limitation becomes the very vessel for unlimited divine expression.

The secret lies not in escaping our humanity, but in making it transparent to transcendence, allowing our hearts to become clear channels through which eternal light might illuminate the world.

The ancient Zohar teaches: "There is no place void of Him, yet He cannot be known."

Perhaps this paradox finds its resolution in this very passage—where the unknowable God makes himself known not through overwhelming glory, but through the intimate experience of His goodness, transforming the sons of God.

The mention of Yahweh 'passing by' Moses in traditional interpretations could imply a sense of separation between God and Moses. However, Yahweh was actually unlocking a different realm within Moses. Unlike on the mountain, Moses wasn't in an ascended state. He, unlike us, did not have Christ within him as "the hope of glory." In contrast, we now have the completeness of Yahweh dwelling within us. Our ascension journey allows us to unlock an awareness of His glory continually. It is through our presence in this world that we can mature in our encounters with Yahweh and collaborate with Jesus in the process of co-creation.

John 1:18 NIV "No one has ever seen God, but the one and only Son, who is himself God and is in closest relationship with the Father, has made him known."

Mirror Translation 1:18 "Until this moment, God remained invisible; now the authentic, incarnate begotten Son, the blueprint of our design who represents the innermost being of God, the Son who is in the bosom of the Father, brings him into full view! He is the official authority qualified to announce God! He is our guide who accurately declares and interprets the invisible God within us."

Jesus in us reveals everything, and because of this, we are no longer in that space where God says, "You'll see my back, for none can see my face and live." It is because His very being now dwells within us as His temple.

"The divine spark within man yearns to reunite with its source, for the light that is hidden within must be revealed"

Colossians 1:27 MIRROR "In us God desires to exhibit the priceless treasure of Christ's indwelling; every nation will recognise him as in a mirror! The unveiling of Christ in human life completes man's every expectation."

Exodus 33:21–23 NIV "Then the Lord said, "There is a place near me where you may stand on a rock. When my glory passes by, I will put you in a cleft in the rock and cover you with my hand until I have passed by. Then I will remove my hand and you will see my back; but my face must not be seen."

The Hebrew for "near me" contains the beginning - את and end. There is a place where, from the beginning to end, you may stand, the realm of infinity.

The Hebrew word for 'rock' literally means a 'title of God'.

Deuteronomy 32:4, we read: "He is the Rock; His works are perfect, and all His ways are just. A faithful God who does no wrong, upright and just is He."

This theme continues in **Deuteronomy 32:15**: "Jeshurun grew fat and kicked; filled with food, they became heavy and sleek. They abandoned the God who made them and rejected the Rock their Saviour."

When Yahweh placed Moses in the rock's cleft, a profound spiritual reality manifested. He positioned Moses spiritually in a place of complete redemption. The scripture then declares, "I will remove my hand, and you will see my back."

In the Hebrew text, the את appears twice here as a marker of divinity. It is used in the phrase "Then I will remove את my hand, and you will see את my back." This connection is significant because it aligns with the divine declaration "I am the Alpha and Omega, the beginning and the end." Therefore, from the primordial beginning to the primordial end, His hand and His back were revealed. This sight encompassed the entirety of creation, from the very beginning to the very end, representing the revelation of completion.

Exodus 34:1–6 NIV The Lord said to Moses, "Chisel out two stone tablets like the first ones, and I will write on them the words that were on the first tablets, which you broke. Be ready in the morning and then come up on Mount Sinai. Present yourself to me there on top of the mountain. No one is to come with you or be seen anywhere on the mountain; not even the flocks and herds may graze in front of the mountain." So Moses chiseled out two stone tablets like the first ones and ascended up Mount Sinai early in the morning, as the Lord had commanded him; and he carried the two stone tablets in his hands. Then the Lord came down in the cloud and stood there with him and proclaimed his name, the Lord. And he passed in front of Moses, proclaiming, "The Lord, the Lord, the compassionate and gracious God, slow to anger, abounding in love and faithfulness,

Exodus 34:27–28 NIV Then the Lord said to Moses, "Write down these words, for in accordance with these words I have made a covenant with you and with Israel." Moses was there with the Lord forty days and forty nights without eating bread or drinking water. And he wrote on the tablets the words of the covenant—the Ten Commandments.

Exodus 34:29–35 NIV When Moses came down from Mount Sinai with the two tablets of the covenant law in his hands, he was not aware that his face was radiant because he had spoken with the Lord. When Aaron and all the Israelites saw

Moses, his face was radiant, and they were afraid to come near him. But Moses called to them; so Aaron and all the leaders of the community came back to him, and he spoke to them. Afterward, all the Israelites came near him, and he gave them all the commands the Lord had given him on Mount Sinai. When Moses finished speaking to them, he put a veil over his face. But whenever he entered the Lord's presence to speak with him, he removed the veil until he came out. And when he came out and told the Israelites what he had been commanded, they saw that his face was radiant. Then Moses would put the veil back over his face until he went in to speak with the Lord.

This outlines two events. Moses received divinely crafted tablets, as recorded in Jewish writings by Louis Ginsberg in "Legends of the Jews." These tablets, fashioned from God's throne, represented direct divine authorship. After being away for 40 days, Moses discovered the Israelites built a golden calf and worshipped it. That act of betrayal filled Moses with righteous anger, causing him to break the holy tablets.

The second event holds great prophetic meaning. After Moses had a mystical encounter in the rocky cleft where God's glorious presence passed by, he received divine instructions to carve new tablets with care. It is as if Moses took the tablets from Yahweh's heart and delicately engraved them, symbolising the significance of the rock and what it represents. This symbolic act reflects the prophetic words of Isaiah and their fulfilment in **Jeremiah 31:33**: "I will place my law within them and write it on their hearts." The transition from Yahweh's divine craftsmanship of the tablets to Moses' skilled hands prophetically signifies the future internalisation of the Word within the sons of God, who are living stones. In the first instance, Yahweh took the sapphire stones from the throne, but in the second instance, he asked Moses to retrieve the tablets, symbolising the intertwining of Moses' heart with Yahweh's as they wrote the tablets together.

The co-authorship of the second tablets, where both God and Moses were involved, is a profound representation of a partnership that intertwines the divine realms. This act foreshadows the eventual reality of the New Covenant, wherein God's law becomes etched within the depths of your being. As Moses experiences the realm of becoming one with the rock, his hands connected to the earthly stone, he carves out the tablets, creating a bridge of divine transference between the heavenly and earthly realms. This sacred moment serves as a prophetic image, resonating with the promise of the covenant's ultimate fulfilment.

This transformation manifests in our current reality. As Peter declares, we are "living stones" and a "royal priesthood." Our constant communion transcends traditional religious practices. Whether in workplace, home or ministry settings, we're called to maintain a continuous awareness of our position in Christ. This isn't about designated prayer times but about becoming living prayer and intercession existing in perpetual divine communion.

The "ascension matrix" of Moses charts this transformative journey. While additional insights exist in extra-biblical sources like the Book of Jasher, focusing on canonical and mystical scripture reveals profound truths often overlooked. When we are conscious of our position, divine glory naturally manifests as we continuously mature as living tablets upon which God's image inscribes.

Every believer's life becomes a living document of divine authorship, co-creating with God as we govern and decree in alignment with His purposes. Like Moses, we are stewards of divine mysteries, our lives continuously writing new chapters in God's ongoing story of redemption, our co-inclusion in Christ as co-creators... as He is, so are we in this world.

Gone are the days of confining our devotion to specific moments, like the solitary hours of prayer at the break of dawn. We must awaken to the realisation that we are living, praying, and ascending beings, continuously attuned to the divine realm. Once this awareness is realised, we find ourselves constantly immersed in the resonance of his voice and the palpable essence of His presence.

We are forever in the position of the burning bush, surrounded by seraphim, with Hebrew letters flowing through us, and angels ascending and descending. This deep truth surpasses time, relevant to every second, minute, hour and day, year-round. We are called to embrace this divine communion, to immerse ourselves in the sensory tapestry of this eternal journey.

The term transcendental encapsulates a realm that lies beyond the grasp of human experience, evoking a sense of awe and wonder. Ascension takes us on a captivating journey through various levels of consciousness, each step filled with a symphony of sights, sounds, and sensations.

As we take on this transformative adventure, our senses become heightened, enabling us to uncover the profound connection to Christ within us. With each ascendant step, our souls soar alongside our bodies, expanding our minds and embracing the full spectrum of spiritual dimensions. Through this process, our awareness intensifies, acting as a compass guiding us towards divine mysteries. It is through this heightened awareness that we unlock the ability to encounter new revelations and learn how to skilfully nurture the presence of God within us.

Ascending your mountain, you ascend the structure entangled in the DNA of Christ before the foundations of the world. That structure is the movement of all things activating and entangling purpose and destiny, creations life force. You are enveloped in a structure entangled in the essence of Christ eternally. Each dimension pulsates with the energy of all creation, intertwining with your purpose and destiny. A flood of primordial memories quickens your spirit, revealing the realm of completeness you shared with Him before the universe came into existence.

As we ascend, our memory of our completeness in him before creation unfolds before you. The words of Jesus echo in your ears, "Did I not say that you are gods?" The air is charged with the weight of this revelation, a revelation that transcends mere understanding. We bask in the knowledge that we are Elohim, divine beings. The sight of ourselves as gods may seem overwhelming, but it is an intrinsic part of our identity. It is time to shed this veil and embrace your divine nature, fully aware of your position in Christ.

Your life is ascending back to its original state, allowing you to believe and pursue immortality.

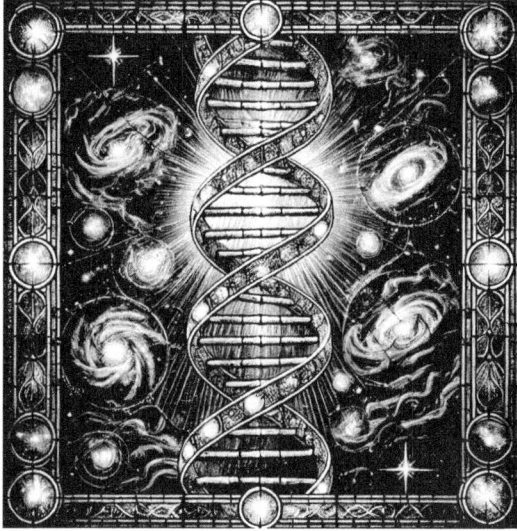

PRACTICAL ASCENSION & MEDITATION ACTIVATIONS

The following ascension meditations serve as guidelines to enhance and enrich your ascension adventure. These meditations were written to help you engage and expand your consciousness. Remember that your ascension is a personal journey, and you are encouraged to customise and expand these meditations according to your comfort level. Times are guidelines, not formulas. Remember, this is your journey with Jesus, so embrace the uniqueness and nurture your own authentic process.

Each ascension will start with a positioning process that I'll post once and you can apply it to each one.

Ascension positioning:

- Find your own ascension space where there is peace and quite and you are able to focus without distractions. Try to sit up straight but comfortable, if lying down works better for you...then cool bananas.

- Scripture anchoring: use relevant scriptures for your ascensions. "Open my eyes that I may see wonderful things in your law" (Psalm 119:18). Lift up your eyes and look from the place where you are..." (Genesis 13:14).

- I like to take communion before intentional ascensions or meditations. Jesus, the cross, the body and blood are my ascension gateways.

- Begin by grounding: Set intention for divine connection. Visualise the breath of Yahweh entangling your spirit. Take deep breaths, in through your nose, out through your mouth. Breathe in peace and release stress, tension and anxiety. Continue the process until you feel your spirit settling into a realm of shalom (peace). Don't be in a hurry. Get the sweet spot.

- I usually have some essential oil like Frankincense in a diffuser going and I ring my singing boil. I engage with the fragrance and the frequency of the sound. 'Frequency aligns you, fragrance ascends you.'

- During your ascension, visualise what you breathe in and what you release. Your imagination creates.

Practical Steps to Meditate and Ascend into the Mystical Realm of Darkness

Entering the Cloud: Initial Meditation

1. Breath Awareness:

- Close your eyes and focus on your breathing. Breathe deeply and slowly, imagining the air around you as divine energy.

2. Visualisation of the Cloud:

- Visualise a bright cloud descending around you, symbolising God's manifest presence (Exodus 19:9).
- Imagine this cloud enveloping your senses, your mind, will and emotions, preparing you for deeper spiritual perception.

3. Scripture Anchoring:

- Meditate on Deuteronomy 4:11, reflecting on the progression from the cloud to the thick darkness.
- Internalise the truth that God calls you to move beyond the surface into deeper spiritual realities.

Stepping Into the Thick Darkness

1. Deepening Awareness:

- As you ascend, imagine the cloud thickening into darkness. This is not emptiness but a sacred space filled with divine potential.
- Contemplate Isaiah 45:3, "I will give you the treasures of darkness and hidden riches of secret places."

2. Focus on Divine Light Within the Darkness:

- Envision a "black fire" blazing within the darkness, representing God's intense presence hidden within mystery.
- Reflect on the paradox of light hidden within darkness (Deuteronomy 4:11).

3. Engage with Silence:

- Allow yourself to be still. In this silence, listen for the "whisper of the heavens" – divine guidance or impressions arising from deep within. Allow the mystery of the darkness entangle your spirit.

Ascension: Encountering the Divine

1. Surrender to Divine Revelation:

- Imagine yourself stepping deeper into the darkness, where layers of divine wisdom and mystery are unveiled.
- Contemplate the Hebrew term *araphel* (thick darkness) as a womb of spiritual rebirth. Allow this imagery to stir a sense of new creation within you.

2. Ask for Divine Secrets:

- In humility and faith, ask God to reveal the treasures of this realm. Wait patiently for impressions, visions, or scripture that comes to mind.

3. Encounter the Supernal Realms:

- Be open to encountering angelic beings, spiritual entities, or divine energies within this space. Allow God to govern the encounter as Moses did.

Integration and Reflection

1. Journal Your Experience:

- After your meditation and ascension, write down any insights, scriptures, or impressions you received.
- Reflect on how these insights can transform your perception of God and your role in His divine plan.

2. Apply Divine Wisdom:

- Consider how the treasures of wisdom you received can be applied in your daily life. This could include strategies for personal growth, work, ministry, or spiritual practice.

3. Repeat and Progress:

- Ascension is a progressive journey. Continue to meditate regularly, moving deeper into this realm of divine mystery over time.

Keys for Success

- **Embrace Uncertainty:** Allow the unknown to stretch your spiritual capacity.

- **Pace Yourself:** Progression into the thick darkness mirrors Moses' journey; it takes time and readiness.

- **Stay Rooted in Scripture:** Anchor your experiences in biblical truths to discern genuine encounters from distractions.

- **Be Led by the Spirit:** Trust the Holy Spirit to guide and protect you throughout this process.

By following these steps, you enter the "thick darkness" as a mystical place of intimacy with God, aligning with His mysteries and discovering the hidden treasures of divine wisdom and purpose.

Activate Levels of Mystical Seeing

Engage ascension positioning.

1. **1. Ra'ah רָאָה (Physical Sight) - Foundation Level**

- Open your eyes and observe your physical space without judgment.
- Notice 3 things you've never seen before in your environment
- Let eyes soften, allowing peripheral vision to expand, you want to capture the current moment.
- See and feel energy starting to shimmer around objects i.e. plants etc.
- Allow recognition to deepen beyond surface level, practice seeing "through" rather than "at" objects.
- Meditate on Moses' experience: "I will turn aside to see this great sight" (Exodus 3:3)

2. **Chazah חָזָה (Prophetic Vision) - Beyond Reality**

"In my vision at night I looked and saw..." (Daniel 7:13)

"The heavens were opened and I saw visions of God" (Ezekiel 1:1)

- Close physical eyes, open spiritual eyes, imagine.
- Imagine a screen of light before your face with portal gates opening, choose a gate to enter.
- Allow colours, symbols, or scenes naturally flow with no control.
- Don't force images, allow them to form and dissolve.
- Notice recurring patterns or symbols.
- Choose a year in your future and focus on images you see recurring in that year.
- Pay attention to sudden "downloads" or insights.

- Practice holding visions without interpreting.
- Practice journaling immediately after to track patterns in your seeing.
- Connect with the prophetic state: "sees a vision from the Almighty, falling prostrate, but having his eyes uncovered" (Numbers 24:4).

3. Hibit הַבֵּיט (Contemplative Gazing) - Transformative Sight

"We all, with unveiled face, beholding as in a mirror..." (2 Corinthians 3:18).

"The Lord would speak to Moses face to face" (Exodus 33:11).

- Choose a sacred object or symbol, like a cross.
- Gaze softly at object without straining.
- Allow object to fill your consciousness.
- Notice how seeing changes you internally.
- Feel transformation occurring through observation.
- Let the object "teach" you. What do you sense is being released through the gazing.
- Stay with sensations of internal shifting. They are waves, jump on and go with the flow.
- Remember the bronze serpent: "When anyone looked at it, they lived" (Numbers 21:9).

4. Shur שׁוּר (Intuitive Perception) - Inner Knowing

"And your ears shall hear a word behind you, saying, 'This is the way, walk in it,' when you turn to the right or when you turn to the left." - Isaiah 30:21

"My son, preserve sound judgment and discernment" (Proverbs 3:21)

- Centre awareness towards your heart.
- Notice subtle feelings, impressions, knowings. What is Jesus

stirring in your heart.

- Trust first impressions without mental analysis.
- Feel information arising from deep within, still focusing on your heart as the centre.
- Practice "seeing" with your whole being i.e emotions, heart. It's like you feel your being has eyes all over. Try to keep the mind separate from heart. They are two different realms, it'll take practice.
- Notice how intuition communicates through your senses channeled through your heart. You want to activate intuition flowing from the centre of your being. To make it easier, you can imagine a divine flow of structure that connects these parts together.
- Visualise in picture form what you sense is flowing from your heart, it activates your heart as the centre of inner knowing.
- Journal impressions flowing from your heart.

5. Tzafah צָפָה (Watchful Observation) - Guardian Sight

"Son of man, I have made you a watchman..." (Ezekiel 3:17)

"I will stand at my watch and station myself..." (Habakkuk 2:1)

- Expand awareness 360 degrees around you
- Feel Jesus protective garment around you.
- Notice spiritual atmospheres and shifts, visualise the shifting.
- Sense the angelic and entities positioned around you.
- Develop strategic awareness of spiritual landscape, what are the details you pick up is shifting.
- Expand your consciousness around these shifting atmospheres constantly engaging your imagination.

- What is Jesus bringing to the fore.
- Shift your energy into the new you are sensing.
- Embody: "I pray that the eyes of your heart may be enlightened in order that you may know the hope to which he has called you." (Ephesians 1:18)

6. Ashar אָשַׁר (Validated Seeing) - Divine Confirmation

Your ears shall hear a word behind you, saying, 'This is the way...'" (Isaiah 30:21)

When the Spirit of truth comes, he will guide you into all truth" (John 16:13)

- Imagine the voice of Yahweh as a frequency picture entangled around your DNA.
- Imagine the frequency of your eyes and ears entangle and become one.
- Breath in the frequency of wisdom (imagine it).
- Focus on something specific in your life you need divine insight for.
- Notice what carries divine "weight" or confirmation in your spirit.
- Let what you imagine align with what you sense in your spirit.
- Practice discerning... true from false impressions are part of the journey.
- Practice hearing of what you are seeing, allowing the sound to expand your eyes.
- Trust confirmed insights completely... connect with the angel of faith in your journey.
- Rest in validation: "So give your servant a discerning heart to govern your people and to distinguish between right and wrong." (1 Kings 3:9)

Sound and Frequency Ascension

(Times are guidelines)

1. Ascension Positioning (10-15 minutes)

2. Sound tuning (5 minutes)

- Begin humming a low, steady tone. It's ok to experiment until you settle in a tone that you feel is activating the sound in your spirit.
- Gradually increase volume. Focus on the sound not as volume but as an activator. At times, I like to use a singing bowl positioned on my hand and as I ring the bowl I breath in the frequency into my body and absorb the vibrations through my hand.
- Continue till you feel vibrations in your body.
- Visualise the sound spiralling up you DNA staircase.

3. DNA Activation (7-10 minutes)

- Focus on your spine as the sound continues.
- Imagine DNA strands illuminating
- Allow each tone to "unlock" cellular memory (Visualise it), you are activating primordial sounds embedded in your spirit. Adjust the sound and tone if need be as you journey to align the physical sound with what you sense the spiritual sound is. It can be different with every activation.
- Feel the energy of frequency moving up through your body.

4. Dimensional Shift (10 minutes)

- Let sound become internal. Focus instead of releasing a sound, you see it moving inward in your spirit.
- Notice spaces between thoughts expanding into pictures of frequency realms. (Those images and how they unfold will be unique to you.)

- Release spiritual awareness. Sound activates the spirit and spiritual entities. Engage with them.
- Open to higher frequencies, feel and elevate your senses to higher realms, hearing or sensing new sounds.

5. Knowledge Reception (10-15 minutes)

- Enter receptive stillness.
- Allow divine insights to flow. Align with downloads into your spirit.
- Notice symbols, formulas, or wisdom arising. (Journal what you see or experience.)
- Remain open without attachment.

6. Integration (5 minutes)

- Slowly decrease sound
- Ground insights into body. Visualise whatever you experienced found a seat into your spirit.
- Connect revelations to daily life.
- Express gratefulness.

Practical Steps and Activations: Engaging the Realm of Sapphire and the Sapphire Throne

The realm of sapphire represents divine revelation, heavenly governance, and alignment with the mysteries of Yahweh. The following steps provide practical activations to connect with the sapphire dimension, access divine revelation, and align with your role as a co-creator in the heavenly realms.

1. **Positioning**

2. **Engage the Sapphire Floor: Visualisation and Alignment**

    - **Ascension into the Sapphire Realm**:

        - Close your eyes and visualise yourself standing at the foot of a great mountain, glowing with radiant blue light. Hear Yahweh's invitation: "Come up here, and I will show you things to come."

        - Begin ascending step by step, declaring with each step: "I ascend in Christ, seated in heavenly places. I set my mind on things above."

    - **Arrive at the Sapphire Floor:**

        - Picture yourself standing before a vast expanse of sapphire, radiating with the brilliance of divine glory. Under your feet is a glowing, translucent blue floor that pulses with the frequencies of the Word.

        - Speak out: "I stand upon the sapphire floor, the foundation of God's throne. I align with His divine order and revelation."

3. **Activate the Aleph-Tav (את): Seeing Through the Divine Lens**
    *   **The Aleph-Tav Revelation**:
        -   Visualise the Hebrew letters **Aleph (א)** and **Tav (ת)** forming a cosmic lens before your eyes. These letters represent the fullness of creation and the multidimensional nature of God's Word.
        -   Declare: "I engage the Aleph-Tav, the beginning and the end. Through this lens, I see beyond the natural realm into the mysteries of Yahweh."
    *   **Ask for Vision:**
        -   "Father, reveal to me what You desire me to see through Your divine lens."
        -   Wait in stillness for impressions, visions, or inner knowing. Write down or record any insights.

4. **Engage the Living Hebrew Letters**
    *   **Encounter the Letters**:
        -   Picture the Hebrew letters dancing before you, radiating light and sound. Each letter emits unique frequencies that form the building blocks of creation.
        -   "I align with the living Hebrew letters, the frequencies of creation. Let their revelation unlock the mysteries of my calling."
    *   **Meditate on Specific Letters**:
        *   Focus on the Hebrew letters סַפִּיר **(Sapphire)**:
        -   **Samekh (ס):** Divine support, surrounding light and ascension.
        -   **Pe (פ):** The mouth, creative expression and breath.
        -   **Yod (י):** God's hand and creative power.
        -   **Resh (ר):** Authority, leadership, divine insight into

original intent.

- Declare:" I engage with סַפִּיר. I receive the wisdom, creativity, and authority embedded in the sapphire realm."

5. Experience the Sapphire Throne

- **Position Yourself on the Throne:**
  - Visualise the throne of God, made of radiant sapphire, surrounded by the rainbow of His covenant. See yourself seated with Christ at His right hand.
  - "I am co-seated with Christ on the sapphire throne. I engage with His authority, wisdom, and governance."
  - Soak up the frequency released from the throne. Feel yourself become one the throne.
  - Sense the spiritual entities embedded within the throne and their movements... engage with them.

- **Engage the Seven Spirits of God:**
  - Picture the seven lamps blazing before the throne, representing the seven spirits of God (Isaiah 11:2):
    - Spirit of the Lord
    - Wisdom
    - Understanding
    - Counsel
    - Might
    - Knowledge
    - Fear of the Lord
  - Ask each spirit to release its revelation into your life.

6. Release Sapphire Frequencies

- **Engage with Creation:**
  - Place your hands on a stone, crystal, or the earth and

declare: "I release the frequencies of the sapphire throne into creation. Let divine alignment, order, and life flow into this realm." You can do that with many objects or aspects of creation.

- **Proclaim Over Situations**:
    - Speak into a situation where you desire heaven's governance and justice to manifest: "From the sapphire throne, I release divine order and justice into [specific situation]. Let Yahweh's will be done on earth as it is in heaven."

7. Record and Reflect

- After the encounter:
    - Write down any visions, impressions, or revelations you received during your engagement.
    - Note practical steps or decisions you feel led to take as a steward of what Yahweh has revealed.

8. Daily Activation of the Sapphire Realm

- **Morning Alignment**:
    - Start each day by declaring: "I stand upon the sapphire floor. I align with the divine frequencies of the throne room and walk in the authority of Christ."
- **Ongoing Engagement**:
    - Meditate on Colossians 3:1–2: "Since I have been raised with Christ, I set my heart on things above, where Christ is seated at the right hand of God."
    - Spend a few moments visualising the sapphire throne and engaging its frequencies. You want to unlock your position in this realm.
- **Partner with Heaven**:
    - Be attentive to moments where God invites you to release

heavenly governance into earthly situations. Speak or act in alignment with what you sense from the sapphire realm.

Final Declaration

Stand with your arms lifted, and proclaim:

"I ascend into the sapphire realm, the foundation of God's throne. I align with the Aleph-Tav, the living Word, and the seven spirits of God. I receive the mysteries of Yahweh and walk in the authority of His divine governance. From the sapphire throne, I release heaven's frequencies into the earth, manifesting His will and glory."

Here is the same activation for Sapphire but incorporating the divine realms of encounter from earlier in the book.

Activating the Realm of Sapphire Through the Four Realms of Divine Encounter

The four realms of divine encounter—**Summons, Divine Positioning, Invocation of Identity, and Worship Dimension**—align perfectly with engaging the sapphire dimension, the realm of Yahweh's throne. Below is a practical framework combining these realms with activations for accessing the sapphire throne's mysteries.

1. The Summons: Ascending to the Sapphire Throne

Scriptural Context:

- *Exodus 19:3*: "Moses went up to God. The Lord called to Moses from the mountain."

- The summons is an invitation into Yahweh's presence, awakening dormant spiritual frequencies.

Activation Steps:
1. Hear the Summons:

  - Sit in a quiet space. Visualise Yahweh's voice calling your name twice (e.g., «John, John») as He did for Moses.

  - Declare: "Yahweh, I hear Your summons. I respond to Your call to ascend into Your presence."

2. Ascend in Spirit:

  - Picture yourself standing at the base of a radiant mountain glowing with sapphire light.

  - Begin stepping upward, whispering with each step: "I ascend into the sapphire realm, where the mysteries of Your throne are revealed."

3. Engage with the Sapphire Frequency:

  - Once you reach the summit, imagine standing on the

sapphire floor. Sense its vibrant blue energy connecting with your spirit.

○ Speak: "I align with the frequencies of the sapphire throne, preparing my being for divine encounter."

2. Divine Positioning: Receiving Authority on the Sapphire Throne

Scriptural Context:

- *Psalm 2:7*: "You are my son; today I have become your father."
- *Hebrews 12:22-24*: "But you have come to Mount Zion..."
- Divine positioning establishes your authority across spiritual dimensions, granting access to govern from Yahweh's throne.

Activation Steps:

1. **Visualise the Sapphire Throne:**
   - Picture Yahweh seated on His throne, surrounded by a brilliant rainbow and blazing lamps (Revelation 4:4-6).
   - See yourself invited to stand before Him.

2. **Receive Your Position:**
   - Hear Yahweh declare over you: "You are My son/ daughter. I establish you with authority in heavenly places."
   - Respond by: "I receive my divine positioning as a co-heir with Christ. I align with Your heavenly government."

3. **Step into the Throne Realm:**
   - Picture yourself seated with Christ on the sapphire throne (Colossians 3:1-2). Sense His authority flowing through you.
   - Declare: "I govern from the sapphire throne, aligned with

Your justice and mercy."

3. Invocation of Divine Identity: Becoming Elohim

Scriptural Context:

- *Psalm 82:6*: "I said, 'You are gods [Elohim], and all of you are sons of the Most High.'"
- *Exodus 7:1*: "See, I have made you like God [Elohim] to Pharaoh."
- This realm awakens your identity as a reflection of Yahweh's image, a son of God operating with divine authority.

Activation Steps:

1. **Engage the Sapphire Letters:**
   - Visualise the Hebrew letters ספיר (Sapphire) dancing around you, forming a divine arc of light.
   - Declare: "I am a living stone, a vessel of ספיר. I align with the wisdom, creativity, and authority of Yahweh."

2. **Awaken the Elohim Nature:**
   - Meditate on John 10:34-36, where Jesus affirms the divine identity of God's sons.
   - Speak: "I embrace my Elohim identity, created in Your image. I reflect Your authority, power, and glory."

3. **Step into Co-Creation:**
   - Picture yourself releasing frequencies from the sapphire throne into earthly situations. Speak life, order, and justice into your surroundings.
   - Example: "From the sapphire realm, I release divine justice into [specific situation]. Let heaven's order manifest on earth."

4. The Worship Dimension: Becoming Worship

Scriptural Context:

- *Revelation 4:8-11*: "Day and night they never stop saying, 'Holy, holy, holy is the Lord God Almighty.'"
- Worship aligns every part of your being with the divine frequency of Yahweh's image, quickening you as a vessel of worship.

Activation Steps:

1. **Prostrate Before Yahweh:**
   - Kneel or lay down, imagining the sapphire floor under you. Feel the vibrations of worship radiating from the throne.
   - Whisper: "Holy, holy, holy is the Lord God Almighty. I align my spirit, soul, and body with the frequencies of heaven."

2. **Engage with the Living Creatures:**
   - Visualise the four living creatures around the throne, their voices harmonising with the heavenly host.
   - Join their worship by singing or speaking your adoration: "You are worthy, O Lord, to receive glory, honor, and power."

3. **Become Worship:**
   - Picture your being merging with the sapphire light, radiating the sound and presence of Yahweh.
   - Declare: "I am an embodiment of worship. My entire being resonates with the frequencies of the sapphire throne."

Bringing the Four Realms Together

1. **Summons**: Respond to Yahweh's call by ascending to the sapphire throne.

1. **Positioning**: Accept your role as a co-heir, seated with Christ in heavenly places.

2. **Invocation**: Activate your divine identity as Elohim, reflecting Yahweh's image.

3. **Worship**: Align your entire being with the frequencies of the throne, becoming a vessel of worship.

Activation Practice for Engaging the Dimensions of Glory

This activation is a **step-by-step guide** designed to take you into the **four dimensions of Yahweh's kavod (כָּבוֹד)**—splendour, honour, wealth, and power described in the passage. Each step includes **specific actions**, **visualisations**, and **declarations** to make your engagement practical and transformative.

1. **Positioning**

2. **Engage the Cloud of Glory**
   1. **Visualise the Cloud:**
      - Picture a **thick, radiant cloud** surrounding you, dense with divine presence. Imagine it pulsating with light, shifting between gold, sapphire, and white hues.
      - Feel the cloud envelops you, pressing against your skin. Acknowledge the Aleph-Tav (את):
      - Within the cloud, see the **Aleph (א)** and **Tav (ת)** as glowing symbols floating before you. They represent the beginning and the end, the fullness of Yahweh's presence.
      - Imagine these letters entering your heart and merging with your spirit.

   2. **Declaration:**
      "I step into the cloud of Your kavod. Jesus, through the Aleph and Tav, you are the fullness of my beginning and end. Open the realms of Your glory to me."

3. **Move Through the Dimensions of Glory**
   Each dimension is a progressive layer within the cloud. Take time to engage deeply with each.

Dimension 1: The Splendour of Yahweh

1. Activate the Illuminating Mirror:

- Visualise a vast, radiant mirror within the cloud. It reflects Yahweh's indescribable beauty and glory, shining directly into your heart.

- Stand before the mirror and see yourself transformed, glowing with Yahweh's light.

2. Meditate on His Splendour:

- Psalm 145:5: "They speak of the glorious splendour of Your majesty."

- Allow your spirit to absorb this light, purifying your thoughts and emotions.
  "I behold Your splendour, Yahweh. Your light transforms me into Your image, radiating Your beauty into creation."

Dimension 2: The Honour of His Glory

1. Step into the Weight of Honour:

- Feel a **cloak of honour** descending upon your shoulders. It is heavy but comforting, a representation of Yahweh's reverence and essence.

- Imagine this cloak grounding you in the eternal truths of Yahweh—the "depth of the beginning and the end."

- There's a realm of forgiveness within honour, entangle with this realm if you sense you need to.
  "I am clothed in the honor of Your kavod. Your eternal nature surrounds me and strengthens me, grounding me in Your essence."

Dimension 3: The Wealth of His Presence

1. Enter the Treasury of Heaven:

- Visualise a **vault of abundance** within the cloud, filled with treasures of both spiritual and material significance—light, wisdom, provision, healing, and peace.
- Reach out in faith and take from this treasury what you need for this time. See it flowing into your hands as golden light or tangible blessings.
- Acknowledge and entangle with the angel of gimmel ג

2. Access the Divine Economy:

- Acknowledge that every blessing flows from Yahweh's presence and manifests into your reality.
- Reflect on one area in your life where you need divine abundance—be it wisdom, finances, relationships, or spiritual growth.
- See they angel of abundance release from the infinite river of provision.
- Imagine the areas being filled and overflow.

3. Practical Step:

- Speak a specific need into the atmosphere and visualise Yahweh meeting it.

4. Declaration: "I receive from the wealth of Your kavod. Your abundance flows freely into my life, aligning every area with Your divine provision."

Dimension 4: The Demonstration of His Power

1. Feel the Power of His Outstretched Arm:

- Within the cloud, see Yahweh's hand extended toward you. As you reach out to touch it, feel a surge of power flowing through you—an infusion of His authority.

- Visualise this power as a tangible force, breaking obstacles and releasing miracles.

2. **Activate Signs and Wonders:**

- Declare Yahweh's authority over a specific area in your life where you need His intervention—healing, breakthrough, or restoration.
- Engage your imagination in every area as you witness Jesus' intervention.

3. **Practical Step:**

- Place your hands on your heart and release Yahweh's power through prayer into those areas.

4. **Declaration:** "I carry the power of Your kavod. Through Your outstretched arm, miracles, signs, and wonders flow, manifesting Your authority on earth."

4. **Seal the Encounter**

1. **Return from the Cloud:**

- Gradually visualise the cloud lifting, leaving behind a glowing light within your heart.
- Feel yourself grounded in the natural world but transformed by your encounter with Yahweh.

2. **Give Thanks:**

- Spend time thanking Yahweh for revealing His kavod to you.

3. **Practical Step:**

- Write down key revelations or insights you received during each dimension.

4. **Declaration:** "Yahweh, I thank You for the journey into Your

kavod. I carry the splendour, honour, wealth, and power of Your glory into every part of my life."

Mystery of 40 Days and מ: A Meditation Practice Guide

This meditation practice draws from the mystical symbolism of Moses' 40-day transformation on Mount Sinai, incorporating the spiritual principles of the waters (מ/mem) to facilitate personal transformation and heightened consciousness. The practice is structured as a 40-day journey, with daily meditation sessions divided between "upper waters" (daytime) and "lower waters" (evening) practices.

Morning Practice (Upper Waters - מ)

1. Positioning

2. Ascension Visualisation (15 minutes)

- Envision a pillar of light extending from crown to infinity
- Mentally recite „אֶהְיֶה" (ehyeh - I AM) with each breath
- Feel yourself ascending through layers of consciousness

3. Upper Waters Meditation (20 minutes)

- Focus on receiving divine wisdom
- Visualise the open מ as a gateway to higher consciousness
- Allow insights to flow down like celestial waters, like waves, catch one andsee where it takes you.

4. Integration (5 minutes)

- Record any insights received
- Set intention for practical application in your immediate environment

Evening Practice (Lower Waters - ם)

1. Positioning

2. Matrix Meditation (15 minutes)

- Focus on the closed ם as the womb of creation
- Feel yourself as a vessel for divine manifestation
- Allow upper and lower waters to merge within, imagine it and allow your imagination to expand the experience

3. Manifestation Practice (10 minutes)

- Bring attention to physical reality, focus on what you received with the open מ and place it in the closed ם.
- Envision how the spiritual insights transform and imagine them in your daily life
- Feel the integration of heaven and earth

Activating the Ascension Gates through the Four Realms of Encounter

This ascension practice focuses on engaging and activating the spiritual gates within, as you journey through the Four Realms of Encounter: **The Summons, Divine Positioning, Invocation of Divine Identity, and Worship Dimension.** These realms, rooted in scriptural revelation, are pathways to unlocking ascension and experiencing deeper union with Yahweh.

Positioning

Meditative Journey Through the Four Realms

1. **The Summons: Responding to the Call**
   - **Focus Scripture:** *"The Lord called to Moses from the mountain."* (Exodus 19:3)
   - **Meditation:**
     - Visualise yourself standing at the foot of a vast, radiant mountain, its peak hidden in the clouds. From the summit, you hear Yahweh calling your name.
     - Let the sound of His voice resonate through you, stirring dormant parts of your being.
     - Breathe in: "Lord, I hear Your call, and I respond. I align with Your voice to ascend into Your presence."
   - **Engagement:** Feel your spirit lifting as you ascend the mountain, leaving behind all distractions and burdens.

2. **Divine Positioning: Entering Your Authority**
   - **Focus Scripture:** *"You are my son; today I have become your father."* (Psalm 2:7)
   - **Meditation:**
     - At the mountain's summit, you stand before Yahweh's throne. Around you are multitudes of angels and

witnesses. Yahweh speaks over you, declaring: "You are My beloved son/daughter. I have positioned you in heavenly places with Christ."

- See yourself being robed in light and crowned with His glory. Feel the weight of authority and sonship resting upon you.

- Silently or audibly declare: "I receive my divine positioning as a son/daughter of Yahweh. I step into the authority of my ascended reality."

- **Engagement:** Let this truth settle into your spirit. Visualise your seated position with Christ, above all earthly limitations.

3. Invocation of Divine Identity: Embodying Elohim

- **Focus Scripture:** *"I have made you like God [Elohim] to Pharaoh."* (Exodus 7:1)

- **Meditation:**

  - Visualise a gateway of light before you, representing the **Petach** (the portal of revelation). As you step through, Yahweh places a seal of divine identity on your forehead with the blood of Jesus.

  - Streams of living water flow from this portal, connecting heaven and earth. You become aware of your role as a bridge between realms—a Jacob's ladder where angels ascend and descend.

  - Silently or audibly affirm: "I awaken to my identity as a reflection of Elohim. I open the ascension gates within me and entangle with Christ's divine nature."

- **Engagement:** Feel your spirit expand as the mysteries of your divine lineage unfold. Allow this awareness to infuse every part of your being. We are sensitive to qualities and abilities being transferred.

4. **Worship Dimension: Becoming Worship**

- **Focus Scripture:** *"The pillar of cloud would come down... and the people worshiped."* (Exodus 33:10)
- **Meditation:**
  - Visualise the **Dalet** (the humble door) opening before you. As you step through, a pillar of cloud descends, surrounding you with Yahweh's presence of awe and reverence.
  - In this sacred space, you are no longer just worshiping—you are becoming worship itself. Every part of your being vibrates with His frequency. Imagine entangling with the vibration and frequency.
  - Silently or audibly declare: "I align my spirit with the sound of Yahweh's presence. I move from worshiping into becoming worship. I am worship."
- **Engagement:** Rest in this resonance. Let it transform you, aligning every dimension of your existence with His divine frequency.

Ascension Integration: Unlocking the Gates

1. **Petach (Revelation Gateway):**

- Visualise a living portal of light that draws you deeper into divine mysteries.
- Declare: "I step through the Petach, opening the gates of revelation to ascend into new dimensions of understanding."

2. **Dalet (Humility Door):**

- See a humble door before you, inviting surrender and intimacy.
- Declare: "I open the Dalet, entering a place of stillness and communion with Yahweh."

3. Sullam (Ladder of Ascension):

- Imagine the ladder of Jacob rising within you, connecting heaven and earth.
- Declare: "I ascend the Sullam, rising through realms of shalom in and through the eternal rest of Jesus."

Sealing the Activation

- **Gratitude:** Take a moment to thank Yahweh for the encounter and the activation of the ascension gates.
- **Declaration:** Proclaim: "I seal this journey in the name of Yeshua. I choose to live from the ascended state, carrying the revelation of the ascension gates into my daily life."

Post-Meditation Reflection

After completing the practice, journal any visions, impressions, or revelations. Note any shifts in your awareness or spiritual perception. As you return to this practice regularly, expect deeper encounters and greater clarity in your ascended reality.

Shalom and blessings as you continue your journey through the gates of ascension!

Activation for Ascension and Crossing Over Through Realms

Positioning

Step 1: Grounding and Opening to the Presence

1. **Invocation**: Speak aloud: "Yahweh, Eternal One, I invite Your Presence into this moment. As Moses sought Your glory and found Your goodness, I open my heart to experience the fullness of Your divine light. I am a vessel of Your beauty, purity, and transformation."

2. **Root Yourself in Creation**: Visualise roots growing from the soles of your feet into the earth, grounding you deeply. Simultaneously, imagine a golden light descending from above, connecting to the crown of your head. Let the light fill your body, merging heaven and earth within you.

3. **Breath Alignment**: With each inhale, imagine drawing divine light into your heart. With each exhale, envision releasing barriers that separate you from the fullness of HIs divine presence.

Step 2: The Mystery of Goodness

1. **Meditation on Goodness (טוּב / ṭûḇ)**: Reflect on the word ṭûḇ, the divine goodness of Yahweh. See this goodness as a radiant, golden light flowing before you.

2. **Visualise the Light of Goodness: Picture** Yahweh's goodness moving like a stream of liquid gold, crossing through your heart. Let it cleanse, heal, and illuminate every corner of your being.

3. **Face-to-Face Encounter (פָּנֶה / paneh)**: Imagine standing face-to-face with Yahweh. See His goodness as a

reflection in your inner being.

"Reveal Your face within me, for You dwell in me as my hope of glory."

Step 3: Crossing Over (עָבַר / ʿā·ḇǎr)

1. **The Pathway of Crossing**: Envision a bridge of light stretching between realms—earthly and heavenly, finite and infinite. Step onto the bridge, feeling each step lighten your spirit. See Hebrew letters running across the bridge igniting transference frequencies.

2. **Declaration: As you walk, proclaim:** "I cross over into Your realms of glory, guided by Your goodness and the indwelling Christ. Proclaim Your name in me."

3. **Feel the Shift:** As you cross, imagine realms of divine mysteries opening within you—layers of your spiritual DNA awakening to the eternal truth of your identity as a co-creator with Christ.

Step 4: Integration and Activation

1. **Receive the Name (יהוה Yahweh)**: Hear the divine name being proclaimed within you. Chant, י, ו, ה, ה Encounter each letter as an ascension realm spiralling upwards.

2. **"Yahweh**, inscribe Your name upon my heart. Let it call forth Your light, Your presence, and Your purpose in me."

3. **Declare Your Transformation:** "I am a living portal of divine goodness. As heaven flows into me, I release heaven into the world. I am transformed to transform, ascending to unite heaven and earth."

Step 5: Co-Creation

1. **Meditate on Christ in You (Colossians 1:27)**:
   Envision Jesus' light radiating outward from within you,
   filling the room, the world, and the cosmos.
   "Christ in me is the hope of glory. His light is my
   completeness, and through Him, I am one with the Father."

2. **Blessing the Earth:** Stretch your hands outward and
   imagine divine light pouring through you into the earth.
   Start blessing and calling forth.
   "As Your goodness crossed over to me, let it now cross
   through me to bless the world. Let the light of Your glory
   illuminate every heart and every realm."

Let us do an ascension into the realm of "I AM WHO I AM" and unlock this sacred space.

Settle yourself, for you are already in an ascended state. You are the mountain, yet you also perceive your mountain separately. Behold the cosmic darkness encompassing the mountain—"darkness was hovering over the surface of the deep." This is the mystery. Take a moment to absorb this darkness, its frequency. Pay attention to what you perceive, what you hear.

Step into this darkness. Remember—Yahweh called from within, and Moses entered; both share the same Hebrew root. You are stepping into His core essence. As you move into the darkness upon the mountain, enter Yahweh's voice. What is its sound? Its appearance? The realm of Yahweh descended, face to face, mouth into mouth.

Envision Yahweh's face. How does He reveal it to you? Witness your face merging into the face of Yahweh. Sensate His breath, His frequency. Feel your face dissolving into His, transitioning through face-into-face communion. Yahweh raises a mirror before you—look at your countenance. Soak up the entanglement with His face. Focus on the sensations in your face. Can you sense the frequency trembling within? The sensation of His face upon yours, His mouth upon yours, His breath within yours?

Now Yahweh unveils an intensified realm of His presence—the realm of "וְהָיֶה I AM WHO I AM"—the place of becoming. Picture it as the burning bush, and step into this spiritual fire. Not earthly flame, but divine—azure, crimson, golden. Experience the spiritual jolt as you enter. Within this realm of "I AM WHO I AM," experience the transforming fire, the divine furnace that melts to transform.

Stay in this moment of transformation. Let Yahweh's fiery

presence consume and transform you completely. How are you experiencing your emotions right now? What shift in perception are you experiencing? Which entities assist in this process? In what way is Yeshua involved in this realm of becoming?

Listen as Yahweh speaks. Note the difference between His voice outside and within this realm of becoming. Pay attention to your body, your spiritual self. See that voice, the sound of "I AM WHO I AM" flowing through your veins, your DNA, the quickening of transformation.

Glance at the thrones arranged around you, with other divine beings seated on them surrounding you, prepared for issuing commands. They are under your assignment. Witness the angels in motion around you - angelic realms activated from this realm of becoming.

Make your way down the mountain. Experience the real essence of "I AM WHO I AM" inside and around you. Experience the darkness and mystery surrounding you. Recognise the angels connected to you and the thrones nearby. Experience the sense of authority and importance rising within you - a true and profound reverence for the Lord. Humility. Notice how the spirit of wisdom intertwines with your mountain.

Picture yourself wandering down the street. Witness the response of the environment - trees, plants, wildlife, birds - all responding to the awakening within you. You are the centre of creation's attention.

Now, open your eyes. See yourself like this daily. The more you frame it, the more you become it. The more you believe it, the more creation shall recognise it.

Embrace the expansion of your spirit as it explores the depths of memory and revelation in the realm of remembrance.

ABOUT THE AUTHOR

With over 20 years of ministry experience and a BA degree in Theology, Scharl is a Christ-centered mystic dedicated to guiding others into the deeper dimensions of sonship and new creation living. Together with his wife, Bianca, he serves as the pioneering leader of "Wells of MEM", a dynamic ecclesia and mystic community-based in Midrand, Johannesburg, South Africa. This community is devoted to bridging ancient pathways with mystical, spiritual practices, fostering authentic transformation and growth. As the founder of the "Throne Room Mystic Academy", Scharl writes and teaches courses that empower believers to embrace their co-creative identity and position in Christ. His passion for the Hebrew language and the mystical depths of faith informs his work as a pastor, podcaster, and ascension coach. Through his writing, teaching, and leadership, he continues to create spaces for spiritual exploration and growth, helping others uncover the profound mysteries of Co-creating in Christ.

info@throneroommystic.com

www.throneroommystic.com

FaceBook:	@throneroommystic
	@Centre stage Christian Church
	@WellsofMem
	@Scharl van Staden
YouTube:	@Throneroommystic
	@TheWellsofMem

NOTES

NOTES

SeraphCreative

Heaven's Heart for Earth

Seraph Creative is a collective of artists, writers, theologians & illustrators who desire to see the body of Christ grow into full maturity, walking in their inheritance as Sons of God on the Earth.

Sign up to our newsletter to know about future exciting releases.

Visit our website: www.seraphcreative.org

Printed in Great Britain
by Amazon

62979533R00127